PLAYING WITH DRAGONS

PLAYING WITH DRAGONS

Living with Suffering and God

ANDY ANGEL

With a foreword by
N. T. WRIGHT

CASCADE *Books* · Eugene, Oregon

PLAYING WITH DRAGONS
Living with Suffering and God

Cascade Books
An Imprint of Wipf and Stock Publishers
199 W. 8th Ave., Suite 3
Eugene, OR 97401

www.wipfandstock.com

ISBN 13: 978-1-62032-647-3

Cataloguing-in-Publication Data

Angel, Andrew R.

Playing with dragons : living with suffering and God / Andrew R. Angel, with a foreword by N. T. Wright

xviii + 120 p. ; 23 cm. Includes bibliographical references and indexes.

ISBN 13: 978-1-62032-647-3

1. Dragons in the Bible. 2. Suffering in the Bible. 3. Suffering—Biblical teaching. 4. Chaos (Jewish theology). I. Wright, N. T. (Nicholas Thomas). II. Title.

BS1199.S8 A532 2014

Manufactured in the U.S.A.

To Gerry and Evelyn

You have modelled living through suffering with God with honesty and faith, a gift for which I am eternally grateful,

and

To Fabi, Sebastian, and Jason

Who walk with me through everything in love and laughter

and

To Luis and Teofila Villalobos and the congregation of Pamplona Baja Thank you for showing this naive *gringo* that it is possible to stop being theologically embarrassed about poverty and suffering, and for teaching him how to look for and find the love and faithfulness of God in it instead
—¡*gracias hermanos!*

CONTENTS

FOREWORD

THE MONSTERS ARE BACK. There was a time when sophisticated Western audiences, whether reading books or watching movies, did not expect to meet the mythical beasts they had perhaps enjoyed when they were younger. But now, with *The Lord of the Rings* and many other examples leading the way, we are all confronting once more the fabulous creatures of our earlier fantasies. On a personal note, now that I have grandchildren to read stories to, I cannot escape dragons. And I hope the new generation will be wiser than my own, and recognize these and similar monsters as vivid and irreplaceable ways of saying things about our world—our *real* world—and enabling us to come to terms with it.

The Bible is a highly sophisticated book, but its kind of sophistication never involved hiding from the myths and symbols of ancient religion. Instead, the biblical writers, in a wide variety of ways, picked up these images and, like a wise counselor exploring a client's dreams, turned them in fresh directions. Sea-monsters, was it? Israel's God had already defeated them. Leviathan, the ancient dragon? God's toy, a creature for the Almighty to play with. Marduk, the powerful divinity of Babylon? Sent packing into an ignominious captivity. And so on.

The New Testament's picture of Jesus, too, evokes these ancient monsters. The Gospel writers seem to walk on the surface of ancient mythology as Jesus walked on the surface of the water, daring Peter—and all of us—to follow him, to conquer our fears, to discover his victory over the dark sea and the creatures, real and imaginary, that it may contain.

In this splendid little book, Andrew Angel offers a guided tour of some of the most important monsters, both in the ancient non-Israelite world, where they played such an important role, and in the biblical writings themselves. In doing so he not only offers us a set of fascinating studies in key texts like the Psalms and the book of Job, revealing depths of lively and energetic meaning where we might otherwise see only florid language. He also offers, discreetly but clearly, ways of addressing the monsters that still haunt us as individuals and as a society. The multi-layered world of ancient imagery is more relevant to our own than we might have supposed. What at first sight might appear the least promising type of biblical material turns out, in this book, to contain some of the richest promises of all. The God of whom the Bible speaks, the Jesus we find in the Gospels, has won the victory over all the monsters. They are important, but they frighten us no longer. This book is thus, at the same time, an in-depth Bible study and an in-depth counseling session. A rare treat.

N. T. Wright, DD
Professor of New Testament and Early Christianity, University of St. Andrews

Formerly Bishop of Durham

PREFACE

NOBODY BELIEVES IN DRAGONS. Or do they? I used to teach teenage boys religion in schools. One summer day when the examination period was over and the school was generally a bit more relaxed, I decided to explore the nature of mythology with my students. So I asked them the question: do you believe in dragons? The responses were amusing.

The students aged around ten or eleven years old found it quite hard to answer at first. Many of them used to believe in dragons when they were younger, as dragons were an exciting part of their fantasy world. Dragons were fun and they did not want to let go of them. Their education, however, was requiring them to distinguish sharply between reality and fantasy and they knew that dragons did not exist. Intellectually they did not believe in dragons but emotionally they really wanted to cling on to them.

The students aged around thirteen and fourteen were bemused at the ridiculous question. It was perfectly obvious to anyone of any intelligence in the modern world that dragons did not exist. Mythology was invented by people who did not have a proper modern education as a way of trying to explain the universe, but that did not make it true.

The students in their late teens were more cautious. In what sense did I mean believe? What kind of truth was I after? They recognized the desire from their childhood years to conquer dragons and be a hero. They were nostalgic for that stage of life in which they could move so easily from the world of reality to fantasy and back, knowing the difference but not caring so much about the difference. *Puff the Magic Dragon* came up and one of them wondered whether drugs might help them back into that world. I made a hasty (and probably fairly weak) attempt at moral education and they bore patiently with me. They did not believe in dragons but thought that the world would be a better place if we all still did.

I had to visit the administrative office at break time. Entertained by the fascinating and lengthy discussions I had just had, I asked some of the secretarial staff the same question. They looked at me as if I were daft. Slowly their faces changed and they began to look puzzled. Then they began to smile. They looked at each other and then they all looked in the direction of the office of a particular colleague. "Yes, we believe in dragons," they replied.

Nobody I spoke to that day really believed in dragons. Nobody really thought that there were enormous, seven-headed, fire-breathing flying lizards that found particular pleasure in capturing helpless princesses and threatening to eat them. However, most of the people I spoke to did think the language of dragons helped them express something about themselves or the world around them. The language of dragons expressed fears and gave opportunity for excitement. The fantasy language of battling dragons gave expression to ambitions, desires, and emotions. The picture of the dragon as a fire-breathing enemy was the perfect ironic characterization of someone people found difficult. The fact that dragon language belongs to the world of fantasy gave expression to broken hope and the yearning for innocence (and perhaps power). Dragons might not exist but they were meaningful.

I did not believe in dragons either and still do not. However, the way people have used this aspect of ancient mythology to express their spirituality intrigues me. For many people today, speaking of dragons can feel a little bit silly even if wonderful conversations sometimes result. I think that some ancients had a far richer language for exploring their spiritual lives partly because they were willing to use and explore this language.

I wish to explore their language in the following pages. Specifically, I am going to look at the mythology of dragons and their demonic counterparts in Jewish and Christian literature from around 1000 BC to AD 300. There are many Jewish and early Christian texts that refer to dragons and the battle God or his angels fight against them. The myth is easily ignored or sidelined on account of its strangeness—and partly on account of the way in which people who are interested in this mythology languish in its lurid images (which can be rather off-putting for the rest of us). However this language is present from the earliest biblical texts to the writing of the New Testament and it can be found in rabbinic writings. Not only is this language present but I suspect we may have something to learn from it.

One of the interesting things about the language of dragons in this Jewish and Christian literature is that it most often occurs in writings where the author is suffering. Somehow this language has helped different people over many years to find a way of expressing their thoughts and feelings about living with suffering and God. It is this that I want to explore in the following pages.

Quite often questions about suffering and God take the form of trying to justify God. We ask how a loving and all-powerful God could possibly allow such a tragedy to happen. We then try to work through the various possibilities. Maybe God is not capable of restraining all suffering. Maybe God does not love as we love. Maybe God has a higher purpose that we cannot see. Maybe God does not exist and this suffering proves it. Different people find different answers and the theological questions persist—not least because there are no easy answers to them.

This is not the way in which I wish to explore the subject. The texts we are going to study (more or less) accept the character of God: that God is good, faithful, trustworthy, just, merciful, and committed to the people who follow him. They also accept the pain and anxiety of suffering. There is no shying away from the realities. Nevertheless, they try to find a way through the experience. The texts give vent to various emotions. They explore what God might or might not be doing. They find creative ways of praying and hoping. Rather than trying to find out why what is happening to them is happening (which is a perfectly reasonable thing to do), they try to find ways of living through what is happening to them and living through it with God. They want to be authentic about reality and authentic about their faith in God. My hope is that as we explore their grappling and living with suffering and God we might find resources for doing the same.

I am aware that anyone writing on suffering runs the risk of being glib. I do not wish to fall into this trap and apologize to anyone who comes away from reading this book thinking I have done so. I have suffered in various ways in life, as has everybody. We all suffer in different ways and to different degrees. I recognize there are many people who have suffered more than I have. However, my own experience of suffering has made me ask the question of how we suffer as well as possible. My religious faith makes me ask that question in the context of God. I hope that by exploring what others have to say about suffering, we can learn more about how to suffer better—if that makes any sense—and I hope my experience and perspective does not detract from your working through the ancient material with your own experiences of pain and suffering and your own questions in mind.

Before proceeding any further I ought to offer a few quick words about how to read this book. I have made an assumption that readers will be familiar with the biblical writings found in the Christian Old and New Testaments. You do not necessarily need to be familiar with them to read the book and engage with it as you can read the texts I discuss as they appear. However, I do discuss a number of texts in depth and I suggest that if you do not know those texts well, you look them up in a Bible and read them through a couple of times as you read that section of this book. Also, keep the biblical text at hand as you read *Playing with Dragons* so you can check what I have written against the text. You will probably get more out of this book that way and you will certainly engage more deeply with the things I discuss.

On another note, you do not need to read the footnotes. Feedback on my last book included discussions with people who felt they were getting bogged down in the footnotes. Once told this was not necessary, they found it a much more engaging read. Others have suggested to me that they really appreciate being able to look things up for themselves and so like the fact the notes are there. This book has been designed to be read without the footnotes. You ought to be able to read the whole text and understand it without reading a single footnote. However, there is not an author on earth who does not make assumptions. Therefore, I have tried to give people access to other ways of reading the material I discuss or access to understanding why I take a different view by including comments on my readings and those of others in footnotes. If you are the sort of reader who likes engaging in the wider discussion and having better access to it, I hope my footnotes serve your purposes well.

My third note concerns other ancient writings. My guess is that not all readers will be familiar with all the texts I refer to in this book. Therefore I have included a very brief introduction to these writings in the Appendix. You will also find details of English translations of these texts here, should you want to read them for yourselves. I discuss and refer to these texts as they help us see that what may sometimes appear odd or marginal in the Bible was part of Jewish culture more widely. Examining the traditions about dragons in wider Jewish and Christian writings can help us to understand what these traditions are doing in the Bible. I hope that those readers who are not really interested in these texts will bear with me where I talk about them. Wherever possible, I put these references in footnotes, but patiently learning about them will help readers to understand the Bible better.

My final note is rather more important. This book does not simply try to reconstruct or discover the meanings of ancient texts. It tries to discover and engage with the spirituality of those texts. I make the assumption that in using the language of dragons to describe suffering, the ancient authors are playing with metaphor and myth in ways that try to give expression to the human experience of faith in God in the face of suffering. I hope I have traced some of the spirituality of these authors in the situations of suffering they faced. I think I have caught glimpses of the ways in which they worked creatively with this language to say what they were feeling and thinking. If I have come anywhere near success in this, then there may be echoes of our own experience in theirs. There may also be parallels between our experiences and theirs. The way in which their experiences echo our own invites us to enter into their reflections on their experiences, and I would like to comment briefly on how we might accept this invitation—should we wish and choose to do so.

Most of the writings I examine in this book are canonical for Christians or Jews (or both). This means they are authoritative. This raises an immediate question of how texts exploring the spirituality of suffering of particular people in particular places at certain points in history are authoritative for *all* people of a religious faith across time. I am not going to offer any attempt at an answer here. However, I would like to sound a note of caution. In reading for this book, I have come across some writers who would recommend that readers follow the example of the biblical writer, which entails (amongst other things) following the emotional and behavioral patterns of, for example, some of the psalmists. These writers can read as if they are saying "in this sort of situation, you should consider feeling and acting like the psalmist here—this is a good emotional and behavioral example." I am not convinced that this is either healthy or possible. Emotions may be traced with honesty and care. They can be channeled, sometimes, with effort and self-control. However, I am not sure any human being can genuinely and life-givingly follow the emotional patterns of another. I am not sure God ever created human beings to work quite like that. My experience is that such use of texts stifles people's growth emotionally and spiritually. So I would ask you to suspend any belief that the authority of biblical writings demands you try to copy the emotional and behavioral patterns of the biblical authors. Hold to the authority of these writings but do so with a freedom that allows you to hear the voices of the biblical authors as they reflect on *their* experiences of God in *their* suffering and to listen to *your own* voice and experiences of God in *your* suffering.

However, the texts do invite us to make comparisons between our experiences and those of their authors. By all means bring your experiences to the table. If you want to, compare and contrast your experiences with those of the biblical (and extra-biblical) authors, but read these texts with freedom. Allow the similarities to emerge and by all means learn from them. Allow the differences to emerge and ask questions. Listen to the emotional and theological questionings and ramblings of our authors and listen to your own. Be honest and allow their own honesty to encourage you to become more honest about your own wrestling with suffering and spirituality. However, do not feel constrained by the directions in which the biblical authors go. You may not be in the same place as Job, who appears driven to sardonic despair, and so it may be inappropriate to follow his example. You may not be in the same place as those psalmists who want to praise God in adversity, and so you may not be up to following their example. There may be excellent examples in what the biblical authors do but you may not be starting from the same place as they are, and so it may be unhelpful to try to retrace their steps and make them your own. On the other hand, retracing their steps might be just what you need. All I would caution you to do is to read the texts with freedom—and preferably with honesty and prayerfulness.

It is also worth noting that I write as a Christian who accepts the canonicity and authority of the Christian Bible. I write with my own personal history and experiences of suffering. Although I have tried hard to read the texts for what they say, I suspect that my own perspective influences my reading at points. I offer this biographical information to you to help you filter and, where necessary, disagree with my readings of texts and see them (and the tradition I explore) more clearly than I have done.

In the main text of the book, we do not dive straight into this material. Biblical dragons are not a common topic of conversation—their ancient Near Eastern counterparts are even less so. Therefore, we begin in chapter 1 with some background information on the myth in the ancient world. This information is designed to be helpful and so is worth reading, but those who wish to get stuck into biblical study might prefer to skim this and move onto chapter 2 (coming back to chapter 1 if necessary later on). Chapter 2 explores how the ancient myth was used in Genesis and Isaiah 40–55, and particularly how it expresses how high a value God attributes to people. Chapter 3 examines different ways of praying through suffering by examining various psalms. Chapter 4 considers how Job uses the myth to give vent to profound reactions to suffering. Much of this material shows people of faith lamenting their suffering before God. Chapter 5 explores how Matthew talks back to this tradition, suggesting that in Christian faith disciples are to expect lament to go hand in hand with discipline and growth in faith. The final chapter of the book brings the discussion together and ponders what we might learn from this ancient myth.

No book is written in isolation and I want to thank everybody who helped me during the writing of this one. Particular thanks are to go to Tom Coopey, Marcus Throup, and Carolyn Lucas, who kindly read the manuscript and commented on it. I have tried to learn from your helpful comments and appreciate your frankness and friendship—long may this continue. I am enormously grateful to my father, Gervais Angel, not only for reading and commenting on the draft but also for his painstaking work in preparing the manuscript for publication. I am most grateful to my old tutor Tom Wright for taking time out of a very busy schedule to write his foreword—this is a privilege and I hope you enjoyed the read. Finally, I want to express my thanks to old friends Luis and Teofila Villalobos and the Anglican church of Pamplona Baja (Lima, Peru), to my parents, Gervais and Evelyn, and my family, Fabi, Sebastian, and Jason, for helping me to see that God can be present in suffering—both small and great, and that God is faithful.

ABBREVIATIONS
OF ANCIENT TEXTS

2 Bar.	*2 Baruch*
1 En.	*1 Enoch*
Jub.	*Jubilees*
3 Kgdms	Septuagint Version of 1 Kings
LAB	*Liber Antiquitatum Biblicarum*
LXX	Septuagint
1 Macc	1 Maccabees
2 Macc	2 Maccabees
MT	Masoretic Text
NRSV	New Revised Standard Version
OTP	Old Testament Pseudepigrapha
Pr Man	Prayer of Manasseh
Pss. Sol.	*Psalms of Solomon*
1QH	Qumran text, *Hodayot*
11Q5	Qumran text from Cave 11
Sir	Sirach
T. Ash.	*Testament of Asher*
T. Jud.	*Testament of Judah*
T. Mos.	*Testament of Moses*

1

BY WAY OF BACKGROUND

So God created the great sea monsters and every living creature that moves, of every kind, with which the waters swarm . . . and God saw that it was good.

Genesis 1:21

Yet God my King is from of old, working salvation in the earth. You divided the sea by your might; you broke the heads of the dragons in the waters. You crushed the heads of Leviathan; you gave him as food for the creatures of the wilderness.

Psalm 74:12−14

Awake, awake, put on strength, O arm of the LORD! Awake, as in days of old, the generations of long ago! Was it not you who cut Rahab in pieces, who pierced the dragon?

Was it not you who dried up the sea, the waters of the great deep; who made the depths of the sea a way for the redeemed to cross over?

Isaiah 51:9−10

And war broke out in heaven; Michael and his angels fought against the dragon. The dragon and his angels fought back, but they were defeated, and there was no longer any place for them in heaven.

Revelation 12:7−8

THERE BE DRAGONS ALL over the Bible. From the great sea monsters of Genesis to the great dragon of Revelation, dragons appear as the Bible opens and closes, and they pop their grisly heads up at various junctures in between. How did they get there and what on earth (or indeed in heaven) are they doing there? Dragons belong within comedy or fantasy. They make strange companions for Abraham, Isaac, and Jacob, for Moses and David, for Jesus and Paul. *Puff the Magic Dragon*, much as we love him, does not belong in the Psalms. The presence of so many sea monsters in Scripture seems strange. So this opening chapter of the book is devoted to answering the first of the questions above: how did so many dragons find their way into the pages of Holy Writ?

Comical as they may be to people today, stories of dragons have abounded in earlier civilizations. The cultures of the ancient Near East were no exception. They told tales of dragons that spoke of threat, conflict, and victory. The dragon presented some sort of threat and a warrior god defeated the dragon and so removed the threat. The plot was clearly popular and arguably continues to the present day in the legend of St. George and the dragon.[1] Below we will re-tell the tales they told in ancient Near Eastern myths, and trace the steps of our dragons as they crept out of these myths and into the pages of ancient Jewish and early Christian literature.

MYTHS FROM THE ANCIENT EAST

The story of the conquest of the dragon occurs in many forms in ancient Near Eastern literature. There are local variations in the myth. However, the hero is normally the storm god. The enemy is often a dragon but it is sometimes pictured as a river or rivers, the sea, or some other demonic beast. The plots in which the actual combat between the warrior god and his or her foe occur differ considerably in detail. Nonetheless they all have the basic plot of the divine warrior hero conquering the demonic and often draconian enemy.

---

1. For fuller studies of the way the myth developed across history see, Forsyth, *The Old Enemy*; Cohn *Cosmos, Chaos and the World to Come*; and Gaster, *Thespis*. The latter is an older study but still very much worth a read.

Enuma Elish

Probably the best known of these myths is the Babylonian story known as the *Enuma Elish*.[2] Trouble is brewing in the courts of heaven. The mother god Tiamat and the father god Apsu have had a row about how to handle their noisy children. Aspu and his vizier Mummu wanted to kill them. Tiamat said that they had to put up with the noise. Apsu and his sidekick decided to go ahead with their plan anyway. One of the children, the god Ea, got wind of this and had Apsu and Mummu murdered in a pre-emptive strike. He is now irritating Tiamat by sending wind and waves over her day and night. Tiamat has been advised to avenge the death of her husband and deal with her wayward son Ea. So she assembles a mighty army of "serpents, dragons, and hairy hero-men, lion monsters, lion men, scorpion men, mighty demons, fish men, and bull men" (*Enuma Elish* I 142–44) under the leadership of her consort Qingu.

Tiamat informs Ea that she is ready for battle. This horrifies him. Having recovered from the initial shock Ea takes counsel from his grandfather Anshar who panics and blames him for creating this mess. Ea tries to face Tiamat with a spell but, realizing that his strategy is hopeless, retreats and suggests Anshar sends somebody else against Tiamat. Anshar sends the god Anu who also retreats. The assembly of the gods lies silent, panicked, and angry. Then Marduk steps up and promises to kill Tiamat provided he is then made king of the gods. In view of the terrifying fact that Tiamat has created an army of "monster serpents, pointed of fang, with merciless incisors" and "filled their bodies with venom for blood" (*Enuma Elish* III 24–26) the gods make Marduk king and send him off to defeat Tiamat.

Marduk gathers his weapons together, including thunderbolts, fire, and various winds. He rides a terrible storm demon (as his chariot) towards Tiamat. They fight in single combat. Marduk captures her in his net and blows an ill wind into her mouth so she cannot close it. He fires an arrow directly inside her that pierces her heart. When they see their mighty matriarch lies dead, her demonic and draconian armies flee before Marduk who kills some of them and takes others prisoner.

Then Marduk splits Tiamat in two and creates the world from her carcass (*Enuma Elish* IV 135–V 64). Tiamat being pictured as the sea (*Enuma*

2. For the full text of this myth, see the translation by Benjamin R. Foster (*COS* 1.111:390–402). For a discussion of the myth and its background, see Jacobsen, *Treasures of Darkness*, 167–69. For an introduction and translation of the *Enuma Elish*, see Foster, *From Distant Days*, 9–51.

Elish VII 71–75, 132–35), Marduk stretches half her waters out above the heavens in this act of creation and the other half of her waters are placed below the earth (*Enuma Elish* IV 139–40; V 54–59).[3] The gods are very grateful and pronounce in praise the fifty names of Marduk.

The Storm God and the Serpent

This Hittite myth comes from ancient Anatolia (modern Turkey). Part of the story is lost but the outline is as follows.[4] When the storm god of heaven and the serpent arrive in the town of Kiškilušša, the serpent kills the storm god. The goddess Inara helps the storm god get his revenge (the myth assumes that the storm god comes back to life). He invites all the gods to a banquet she prepares. Meantime, she asks the mortal Ḫupašiya to help her. He agrees to this provided she sleeps with him, which she does. She prepares the banquet for the gods and hides Ḫupašiya until the gods are enjoying the party. The serpent and his progeny become sufficiently bloated at the banquet that they cannot get back into their hole. Ḫupašiya appears and ties them up. The storm god comes in and kills the serpent. Then Inara builds a house outside Tarukka and settles Ḫupašiya there, ordering him not to look out of the window. He does and hankers after his wife and children. The full text of the next section does not survive but it seems that Inara gets incensed by Ḫupašiya whining about missing his family and kills him.

The later version of this myth adds some extra color.[5] When the serpent defeats the storm god, he takes out his eyes and heart. So the storm god settles on a ruse. He marries the daughter of a pauper and they have a son who marries the daughter of the serpent. The storm god instructs his son to demand his eyes and heart back from the serpent. He does so and carries the missing organs back to his father. Restored to full health, he returns to the sea where he battles the serpent and kills it.

---

3. For Tiamat representing the sea, see also Jacobsen, *Treasures of Darkness*, 169.

4. For the text of the myth, see the translation by Gary Beckman (*COS* 1.56:150–51). For a brief introduction to the story, see Green, *Storm-God*, 147–51.

5. The text of this later version can also be found in the translation by Gary Beckman (*COS* 1.56:150–51).

The Myth of Baʻlu and Yammu

The closest of these stories both in time and location to biblical texts is probably the myth of Baʻlu and Yammu. This tale comes from Ugarit (modern Ras Shamra in Syria) from about 1400 BC. Parts of the text are missing and so piecing together the story can prove difficult in places. However scholars generally agree on the basic outline.[6]

The high god ʼIlu summons the goddess ʻAnatu and the craftsman god Kôṯaru-wa-Ḫasīsu. When the gods are gathered in council, messengers from the sea god Yammu (also called Ruler Naharu) demand that they give up Baʻlu so that Yammu might steal his gold. ʼIlu tells the messengers that Baʻlu will bring tribute to Yammu and delivers him to the messengers as their prisoner.

Baʻlu is furious and grabs a weapon. ʻAnatu tries to restrain him, advising him that Yammu is too strong for him. But Baʻlu swears to destroy Yammu and Yammu hides under his throne in fear. Kôṯaru-wa-Ḫasīsu pronounces that Baʻlu will become king eternally. He makes a mace, Yagrušu or "Drive Out," with which Baʻlu strikes Yammu on the upper body. Yammu is strong and this does not defeat him. Kôṯaru-wa-Ḫasīsu provides Baʻlu with another mace, ʼAyyamurru or Expeller, with which Baʻlu strikes Yammu on the head. Yammu falls to the ground and Baʻlu sets about tearing him apart. A temple is built for Baʻlu who roars from heaven with his thunder and makes the earth tremble at his voice.

The fragmentary nature of the text leaves the story with some rough edges. Another part of the text speaks of Baʻlu as defeating "Lôtan, the fleeing serpent . . . the twisting serpent, the close-coiling one with seven heads" rather than defeating Yammu/Ruler Naharu (*KTU* 1.5 i 29–30).[7] Elsewhere ʻAnatu makes the claim:

> I have smitten ʼIluʼs beloved Yammu, I have finished off the great Naharu. I have bound the dragonʼs jaws, have destroyed it, have smitten the twisting serpent, the close coiled one with seven heads. (*KTU* 1.3 iii 39–41)[8]

---

6. For the full text of this myth, see the translations by Dennis Pardee (*COS* 1.86:241–74) and Nicholas Wyatt, *Religious Texts*, 34–146. For detailed discussion of the myth, see also Smith, *Baal Cycle*, 1–114.

7. For translation, see *COS* 1.86:265.

8. For translation, see *COS* 1.86:252.

Despite these slight incongruities, the outlines of the divine warrior pattern of myth may be seen. Ba'lu plays the part of the storm god. Not only does he thunder from heaven and make the mountains tremble (*KTU* 1.4 vii 28–35) but he rides the clouds as a chariot (e.g., *KTU* 1.4 v 60). He defeats his enemies who are Yammu and Ruler Naharu. Yammu translates as "sea" and Naharu translates as "river." Ba'lu defeats an enemy god pictured as waters. The foes of Ba'lu are also depicted as the serpent Lôtan, whose seven heads suggest he is some kind of dragon or mythical monster. The descriptions "close-coiling" and "twisting serpent" identify the enemy of Ba'lu as the enemy of 'Anatu. She describes this enemy as a dragon and identifies it with Yammu and Naharu. So this myth depicts the storm god Ba'lu (and his consort 'Anatu) defeating their enemies who are variously depicted as the sea, a river, and a seven-headed twisting serpent or dragon.

The similarities with the Hittite myth of the storm god and the serpent are apparent. The two adversaries are the storm god and a serpent god. That the storm god goes to the sea to defeat the serpent suggests an association between the serpent and the sea. Rivalry exists between the two but the storm god vanquishes the serpent in the end. The *Enuma Elish* follows the same pattern. Marduk rides the storm and fights with the elements of the storm, thunders, and winds. Tiamat takes the form of the sea and her army consists of dragons, serpents, and other demonic mixed beasts. Marduk fights Tiamat and beats her in battle.

So ancient Near Eastern myths were a fertile breeding ground for dragons. Moreover, for all their individuality and differences in detail, these myths follow the same broad outline. The serpent god or dragon or sea or other form of chaotic waters pose a threat or lay down a challenge. This is perceived as evil by the storm god. The storm god meets the challenge by battling the sea god or dragon and vanquishing them. These myths are by and large earlier than biblical writings and so it is almost certain that dragons migrated from these myths and into the Bible. So when they snuck into Scripture, what did they do there?

WHEN DRAGONS SNUCK INTO THE BIBLE

Elements of this ancient Near Eastern mythical pattern can be found in biblical texts.[9] However, the version of the myth in these writings is different.

---

9. The classic study of this mythology in biblical literature is Hermann Gunkel, *Chaos and Creation*, which compares biblical myth with Babylonian myth. A more recent study

The stories of the *Enuma Elish*, the myth of Ba'lu and Yammu, and the Hittite story of the Serpent are precisely that, stories. The myth never really occurs as a story in biblical writings. At best it occurs as an extended scene from a wider story. Most often it appears in fragmentary form. Scenes from the story pop up in texts and although the texts do not tell the whole tale, these snippets are unmistakably derived from the wider story of God defeating the dragon or chaos waters. Often these fragments are like flashbacks to particular scenes in the wider story. The reader who knows the ancient myths gets the impression that the Hebrew writers just assumed that everybody was familiar with the story and they liked to use it creatively. The dragons move from center stage and begin to take on cameo roles.

Probably the closest we come to a full version of the story is found in Psalm 18. In this song of thanksgiving the psalmist praises God as his rock and for enabling him to defeat his enemies. After initial cries of praise, the psalmist offers this testimony (Ps 18:4–16):

> The cords of death encompassed me; the torrents of perdition assailed me; the cords of Sheol entangled me; the snares of death confronted me. In my distress I called upon the LORD; to my God I cried for help. From his temple he heard my voice, and my cry to him reached his ears. Then the earth reeled and rocked; the foundations also of the mountains trembled and quaked, because he was angry. Smoke went up from his nostrils, and devouring fire from his mouth; glowing coals flamed forth from him. He bowed the heavens, and came down; thick darkness was under his feet. He rode on a cherub, and flew; he came swiftly upon the wings of the wind. He made darkness his covering around him, his canopy thick clouds dark with water. Out of the brightness before him

that updates Gunkel and makes use of parallels with Canaanite myth is Day, *God's Conflict*. Recently David Tsumura (*Creation and Destruction*) and Rebecca Watson (*Chaos Uncreated*) have disputed the extent to which ancient Near Eastern myths have influenced biblical writings and seek to demonstrate that it had little to do with creation in Israelite tradition. However, both authors accept the presence of a myth of God fighting the dragon in biblical texts. Tsumura (*Creation and Destruction*, 191–95) admits that at least the figures of Rahab and Leviathan (Pss 74:13–14; 89:9–10; Job 3:8; Isa 27:1) demonstrate the presence of a myth in biblical texts like ancient Near Eastern dragon myths. Watson (*Chaos Uncreated*, 166–68, 186–89) also admits the presence of a Hebrew myth in Psalms 74 and 89 that speaks of God defeating the dragon. Given that neither author has been able to disprove the presence of the myth in biblical texts, it is reasonable to work with the assumption that the biblical writers knew of this myth. There is no need to engage further here with some of the more questionable arguments they offer or with Watson's concerning presupposition that biblical literature can be read in isolation of other ancient literature and be fully and properly understood.

there broke through his clouds hailstones and coals of fire. The LORD also thundered in the heavens, and the Most High uttered his voice. And he sent out his arrows, and scattered them; he flashed forth lightnings, and routed them. Then the channels of the sea were seen, and the foundations of the world were laid bare at your rebuke, O LORD, at the blast of the breath of your nostrils. He reached down from on high, he took me; he drew me out of mighty waters.

This narrative clearly tells the story of the storm god defeating the watery enemy. The psalmist cries out that they are close to death and calls on God. God hears the cry of the psalmist and shakes the world's foundations in anger at their predicament. God fumes and breathes fire. God descends from heaven on an angel and the wings of the wind for battle against the watery foe. On approaching the waters God fires lightning arrows, hailstones, and coals of fire but the battle never takes place. Before God arrives the sea has already fled away in defeat, leaving bare its channels and the foundations of the world.[10] God reaches down and saves the psalmist from the waters of chaos and death.[11] The psalmist is really speaking of God saving him from his earthly enemies in local battles (v. 17) and their language is full of vibrant mythology. The psalmist depicts this event in the language of theophany (as it is often called) to highlight their belief that God was involved in saving them from their enemies.

However, this scene is hardly a story in the way that the Babylonian or Canaanite myths are. It lacks the plots, with all their twists and turns, that are found in the Babylonian and Canaanite myths. It also lacks the delightful way in which they develop their characters over the telling of the story. The theophany of God with all his thunder and lightning may be very impressive but the characterization of Yammu and Tiamat with her demonic hordes is much more colorful than that of the sea in Psalm 18, which has slunk away before we even get to see it (vv. 14–15). Doubtless

10. The motif of fleeing chaos waters is known to the tradition (e.g., Pss 104:7, 114:3; *T. Mos* 10:6). The laying bare of sea beds and river beds (e.g., Isa 44:27; 50:2; Nah 1:4; *LAB* 10:5) is a reference to the fact that the chaos waters have already fled in fear from God the divine warrior. The point of the motif is not always appreciated by commentators, e.g., Craigie who has God rebuke the sea bed (*Psalms 1–50*, 174). The *sea*, not the sea bed, is the mythical enemy. Arriving to an empty sea bed rather playfully emphasizes the power and majesty of God as the sea was not going to hang around to find out exactly how painful defeat would be. It quit while it had time. The *Liber Antiquitatum Biblicarum* of Pseudo-Philo is found in the Pseudepigrapha.

11. Kraus, *Psalms 1–59*, 260–61; Craigie, *Psalms 1–50*, 173–74.

part of the reason for this is that the psalmist wants to glorify God. So the scene moves from the psalmist in peril to God's glorious actions to save the psalmist. By the time we come to a mention of the sea, it has already fled in terror—so that people can see the power of God.

Even though the battle scene of the story is told in some detail, we need to know the wider story to get the impact of this scene here. The audience only understands the irony of the sea having already fled (and so the greatness of God) because they already know that in these stories gods battle seas and that the battle is normally a struggle. This scene assumes some kind of prior knowledge of the ancient myth with which the psalmist plays to make this point about the power of God, and without which the point would be lost.

The same is true for the vision the prophet Habakkuk has of God in the heavenly chariot fighting the chaos waters with arrows and a flashing spear (Hab 3:3–15):

> God came from Teman, the Holy One from Mount Paran. His glory covered the heavens, and the earth was full of his praise. The brightness was like the sun; rays came forth from his hand, where his power lay hidden. Before him went pestilence, and plague followed close behind. He stopped and shook the earth; he looked and made the nations tremble. The eternal mountains were shattered; along his ancient pathways the everlasting hills sank low. I saw the tents of Cushan under affliction; the tent-curtains of the land of Midian trembled. Was your wrath against the rivers, O LORD? Or your anger against the rivers, or your rage against the sea, when you drove your horses, your chariots to victory? You brandished your naked bow, sated were the arrows at your command. You split the earth with rivers. The mountains saw you, and writhed; a torrent of water swept by; the deep gave forth its voice. The sun raised high its hands; the moon stood still in its exalted place, at the light of your arrows speeding by, at the gleam of your flashing spear. In fury you trod the earth, in anger you trampled nations. You came forth to save your people, to save your anointed. You crushed the head of the wicked house, laying it bare from foundation to roof. You pierced with their own arrows the head of his warriors, who came like a whirlwind to scatter us, gloating as if ready to devour the poor who were in hiding. You trampled the sea with your horses, churning the mighty waters.

Alongside Psalm 18, this passage from Habakkuk represents the most sustained description of God's riding out to battle against the forces of chaos in biblical writings before the second century BC. As God approaches the battle, mountains and hills shatter in the path of his chariot. The deep cries out in fear before God tramples it in victory. The elements of the battle scene of the story are all there and in great poetic detail.[12] However, this scene from the story, which constitutes the greater part of a hymn of praise (Hab 3:2–19), is not set within a wider story of why God has come out against this watery enemy and what God achieves through this victory. This lack of clear setting has given rise to many and varied understandings of what the story means, and why it is included in the book of Habakkuk.[13] One thing that does seem clear, however, is that the author was working with a traditional story the original audience would have understood.[14]

12. Andersen, *Habakkuk*, 315–41; Smith, *Micah–Malachi*, 115. For further discussion see Day, *God's Conflict*, 104–9.

13. See Andersen, *Habakkuk*, 259–61 for a review of different perspectives on this matter.

14. Ibid., 350–55. This myth appears in later Jewish and Christian writings both inside and outside the Bible. The *Testament of Moses*, a Jewish text completed in roughly the same era as the New Testament, tells the same story (*T. Mos* 10:1–8a):

> And then his kingdom will appear throughout his whole creation. And then the devil will have an end, and sorrow will be led away with him. Then the hands of the messenger, who is stationed in the highest place, will be filled. He will avenge them of their enemies immediately. For the heavenly one will arise from his kingly throne, and he will go forth from his holy habitation with indignation and wrath on behalf of his sons. And the earth will tremble, it will be shaken violently right to its very ends. And the high mountains will be made low, and they will be shaken violently, and enclosed valleys will cave in. The sun will not give its light. And the horns of the moon will turn to darkness and they will be broken in pieces, and the whole thing will be turned to blood. And the orbit of the stars will be thrown into disorder. And the sea will recede all the way to the abyss, and the springs of the waters will withdraw, and the rivers will be terrified, because God Most High will surge forth, the Eternal One alone. In full view will he come and punish the nations, and he will destroy their idols. Then you will be happy, O Israel!

The story here is substantially the same as in the earlier texts. God leaves his heavenly dwelling place to come and rescue the people of Israel. The language in which this is depicted in these verses has the earth reeling and falling apart as God comes in glory. The heavenly bodies fall out of their places and the mythical enemy, the sea, flees in fear and dread at the coming of God Most High. The end result of the cosmic upheaval and battle against chaos is actually the salvation of Israel. The translation here is taken from Angel, *Chaos*, 119. The *Testament of Moses* is found in the Pseudepigrapha.

Alongside these more sustained descriptions of God's battle with the forces of chaos, there are places where the battle scene is captured in just a few lines of poetry. The book of the prophet Nahum begins with such a scene (Nah 1:3–6):

> The Lord is slow to anger but great in power, and the Lord will by no means clear the guilty. His way is in the whirlwind and the storm, and the clouds are the dust of his feet. He rebukes the sea and makes it dry, and he dries up all the rivers; Bashan and Carmel wither, and the bloom of Lebanon fades. The mountains quake before him, and the hills melt; the earth heaves before him, the world and all who live in it. Who can stand before his indignation? Who can endure the heat of his anger? His wrath is poured out like fire, and by him the rocks are broken in pieces.

God comes in the storm with the clouds at his feet (possibly a reference to coming in a cloud chariot).[15] Just as in Psalm 18 and similarly to the myth of Ba'lu (*KTU* 1.4 vii 25–39) the earth convulses before God. God defeats the chaos waters, rebuking them and drying them up.[16]

Scenes like these in the Psalms, prophets, and later apocryphal and pseudepigraphical writings demonstrate that Jews and early Christians would have been familiar with a story in which God arises from his dwelling and comes to earth in glory. God rides on or in clouds, thundering and shooting lightning at the enemy. The enemy takes the form of the sea, or sea and rivers, or one or more dragons. God defeats the enemy and is enthroned in the temple or heavenly courtroom. In some texts only fragments of this story appear. Whilst they are clearly part of this story, in and of themselves they only picture a single action or point in the story, or a very truncated scene of the wider myth.

Many of these fragments offer nothing more than a snapshot of a scene in the story. These snapshots might be taken at any point in the story but tend to focus on certain scenes. Many capture views of the theophany of God riding on the cloud chariot. One psalmist calls the worshipping community to "sing to God, sing praises to his name; lift up a song to him who rides upon the clouds" (Ps 68:4) echoing the description of Ba'lu in the Ugaritic myths (*KTU* 1.4 iii 15).[17] Another psalmist offers the same picture in slightly more detail (Ps 104:1–4):

15. Christensen, *Nahum*, 181–2.

16. Ibid., 181–93.

17. Tate, *Psalms 51–100*, 176. The text critical issues surrounding the original text of

> Bless the LORD, O my soul. O LORD my God, you are very great. You are clothed with honor and majesty, wrapped in light as with a garment. You stretch out the heavens like a tent, you set the beams of your chambers on the waters, you make the clouds your chariot, you ride on the wings of the wind, you make the winds your messengers, fire and flame your ministers.

Glorious and majestic, God establishes his throne room over the defeated chaos waters and rides out on a cloud chariot accompanied by winds and lightning. The psalmist pictures the Lord as God of the storm going out to defeat the waters of chaos, which, as it happens, God does a little later in the psalm.

Some fragments focus on the convulsions of the earth and heavens at the advent of the divine warrior. The prophet Isaiah pictures the whole universe thrown into convulsion as the Lord God marches from heaven to earth to judge the king of Babylon (Isa 13:9–13):

> See, the day of the LORD comes, cruel, with wrath and fierce anger, to make the earth a desolation, and to destroy its sinners from it. For the stars of the heavens and their constellations will not give their light; the sun will be dark at its rising, and the moon will not shed its light. I will punish the world for its evil, and the wicked for their iniquity; I will put an end to the pride of the arrogant, and lay low the insolence of tyrants; . . . I will make the heavens tremble, and the earth will be shaken out of its place, at the wrath of the LORD of hosts in the day of his fierce anger.[18]

---

this psalm are numerous and Hossfeld and Zenger (*Psalms 2*, 158) suggest an original text that misses the reference to riding on the clouds, but they do accept the image of God riding across the heavens in Ps 68:34 (*Psalms 2*, 159).

18. A similar scene of the shaking of the universe and all its inhabitants can be seen in a much later apocalyptic work (*1 En.* 1:4–9):

> The Great Holy One will come forth from his dwelling, and the eternal God will tread from thence upon Mount Sinai. He will appear with his army, he will appear with his mighty host from the heaven of the heavens. All the watchers will fear and quake, and those who are hiding in all the ends of the earth will sing. All the ends of the earth will be shaken, and trembling and great fear will seize them [the watchers] unto the ends of the earth. The high mountains will be shaken and fall and break apart, and the high hills will be made low and melt like wax before the fire. The earth will be wholly rent asunder, and everything on earth will perish, and there will be judgment on all. With the righteous he will make peace and over the chosen there will be protection, and upon them will be mercy. They will all be God's, and he will grant them good pleasure. He will bless them all, and he will help them

This scene is terrifying. God comes in majesty surrounded by his army of angels in order to execute judgment on those who have sinned. However, when God punishes Babylon, it means freedom and peace for the people of God.

Some fragments picture the point in the story where God defeats the dragon and the sea. Psalm 74 laments the destruction of the temple in Jerusalem (probably by Babylonian soldiers in 586 BC).[19] Part way through the psalmist reminds God of his kingship over creation in the following words (vv. 13–17):

> You divided the sea by your might; you broke the heads of the dragons in the waters. You crushed the heads of Leviathan; you gave him as food for the creatures of the wilderness. You cut openings for springs and torrents; you dried up ever-flowing streams. Yours is the day, yours also the night; you established the luminaries and the sun. You have fixed all the bounds of the earth; you made summer and winter.

God crushes heads of the dragons. One dragon is singled out and named, Leviathan. This particular dragon is probably to be identified with the dragon Lôtan of the Ugaritic texts (the three key "letters" of the Ugaritic word, *l-t-n*, appear in the Hebrew word Leviathan also).[20] More evidence that the Ugaritic Lôtan changed its name to Leviathan when crossing the border into the Bible appears elsewhere. Isaiah describes Leviathan as "the fleeing serpent, Leviathan the twisting serpent, . . . the dragon that is in the sea" (Isa 27:1). Several hundred years earlier, the writer of the Ugaritic myth described Lôtan in the very same words, "Lôtan, the fleeing serpent . . . the twisting serpent, the close-coiling one with seven heads" (*KTU* 1.5 i 29–30). Leviathan (formerly Lôtan) gets around quite a bit as it also probably reappears in the seven headed dragon of Revelation 12.[21]

----

all. Light will shine upon them, and he will make peace with them. Look, he comes with the myriads of his holy ones, to execute judgment on all, and to destroy the wicked, and to convict all humanity for all the wicked deeds that they have done, and the proud and hard words that sinners spoke against him.

The book of 1 *Enoch* may be found in the Pseudepigrapha. The translation here is taken from Nickelsburg and VanderKam, *New Translation*, 19–20.

19. Hossfeld and Zenger, *Psalms 2*, 243–44; Tate, *Psalms 51–100*, 246–47.

20. Hossfeld and Zenger, *Psalms 2*, 247; on the relationship between the names Lôtan and Leviathan, see the article by Day, *Leviathan*, 295.

21.. Aune, *Revelation 6–16*, 684; Day, *God's Conflict*, 24.

Elsewhere the book of Isaiah identifies a monster called Rahab (Isa 51:9): "Awake, awake, put on strength, O arm of the Lord! Awake, as in days of old, the generations of long ago! Was it not you who cut Rahab in pieces, who pierced the dragon?" The prophet recalls the picture of the ancient action of God who battled the dragon, piercing it and cutting it into pieces. (This is not unlike the picture of Marduk splitting Tiamat into two pieces in the *Enuma Elish*.) It is not entirely clear whether the dragon is named Rahab or Rahab battles God alongside the dragon.[22] Either way Rahab is clearly a monstrous enemy of God in this mythical struggle. The prophet continues by associating the defeat of the dragon with the drying up of the sea (Isa 51:10): "Was it not you who dried up the sea, the waters of the great deep?"[23] The defeat of the dragon and the sea occur in parallel, just as in Psalm 74. Rahab is pictured as leading a demonic army in one of Job's laments (Job 9:13): "God will not turn back his anger, the helpers of Rahab bowed beneath him."[24] The helpers of Rahab bow beneath God, either cowering in fear at their imminent destruction or possibly after God has taken them captive. This image of Rahab with her band of helpers recalls Tiamat with her army of demonic creatures.

Some fragments focus on the defeat of the forces of chaos. This defeat may take many forms. God kills the monsters in many texts. Psalm 74 and Isaiah 51 speak of the crushing of the heads of Leviathan and the piercing of Rahab respectively. Daniel recounts the putting to death and burning of the fourth beast (Dan 7:11b). Later Jewish and Christian texts like the *Testament of Asher* and the *Psalms of Solomon* both recall earlier tradition in picturing God breaking the head of the dragon (*T. Ash.* 7:2–3; *Pss. Sol.* 2:25–26).[25] But death is not the only fate depicted.

Other Jewish texts offer a glimpse of the chaos waters fleeing in terror from the divine warrior and so the channels of the deep dry up.[26] The

22. Goldingay and Payne, *Isaiah 40–55*, 2:236; Blenkinsopp, *Isaiah 40–55*, 331–33; Baltzer, *Deutero-Isaiah*, 356–57. Both Blenkinsopp and Baltzer write as if Rahab and the dragon are distinct figures. Day (*God's Conflict*, 91–93) seems to assume that Rahab is the dragon.

23. Baltzer, *Deutero-Isaiah*, 357.

24. Clines, *Job 1–20*, 233; Hartley, *Job*, 173; Habel, *Job*, 192.

25. Angel, *Chaos*, 84, 114. The *Testament of Asher* and the *Psalms of Solomon* may be found in the Pseudepigrapha.

26. The motif of the drying up of the chaos waters in Hebrew tradition seems to reflect the Ugaritic myth where Astarte cries out to Ba'lu to dry up the captive Prince Yammu (Sea) and Judge Nahar (River) (*KTU* 1.2 iv 29–30).

Testament of Moses has the waters of chaos run from the divine warrior in dread (*T. Mos* 10:6). Pseudo-Philo plays with this tradition in his re-telling of the story of Moses dividing the Red Sea (*LAB* 10:5):[27]

> And God said, "since you have cried out to me, lift up your rod and smite the sea, and it will be dried up." Moses did all this and God rebuked the sea and it dried up. And the streams of water stood up and the depths of the earth became visible, and the foundations of the world were laid bare by the fearful roar of God and by the breath of the anger of the Lord.

The story is lightly touched with language and images of our myth. God rebukes the waters of chaos to defeat them in the Bible (e.g., Ps 104:7).[28] The image and language of the roar and breath of God laying bare the foundations of the world and making the depths of the earth visible reflect the language and imagery of Psalm 18:16.[29] The story of God drying up the sea becomes the story of God defeating chaos.[30]

Certain fragments of the myth recall the imprisonment of the monsters. Where Job asks God whether he (Job) is the sea or a dragon that God sets a guard over him, he is clearly familiar with a myth in which God has the chaos monster imprisoned (Job 7:12).[31] The *Prayer of Manasseh* addresses the Lord God Almighty who "shackled the sea by the word of your command, who confined the deep and sealed it by your fearful and glorious name" (Pr Man 3).[32] The images of shackling and confinement depict the imprisonment of the chaos sea.[33] These images seem to merge with another

---

27. Pseudo-Philo's *Liber Antiquitatum Biblicarum* may be found in the Pseudepigrapha. The translation here is taken from Angel, *Chaos*, 164–65.

28. Day, *Conflict*, 57.

29. See further Angel, *Chaos*, 165; Jacobson, *Pseudo-Philo*, 441.

30. Some would suggest that this is the origin of the Red Sea Story, e.g., Kloos, *Yhwh's Combat*. However, I find it difficult to believe that a tradition like the exodus from Egypt, which is so deeply embedded in the texts of ancient Israel (many of which are not at all mythological, e.g., Exod 14), can simply be traced back to some creative author deciding on behalf of the whole community that they would fabricate a history for themselves out of the myth they used to celebrate the work of God in their lives. If the myth was good enough to use to celebrate this work of God without any reference to the Exodus story (as it is in many psalms, e.g., Psalm 46), is there any evidence that anyone felt the need to fabricate a history for the community out of the myth?

31. Clines, *Job 1–20*, 188–90.

32. The *Prayer of Manasseh* may be found in the Pseudepigrapha.

33. Angel, *Chaos*, 82.

biblical image in which the shores of the sea are depicted as the boundaries God has set to prevent the sea engulfing creation and turning it back to chaos. The prophet Jeremiah evokes this image, speaking in the voice of God: "I placed the sand as a boundary for the sea, a perpetual barrier that it cannot pass; though the waves toss, they cannot prevail, though they roar, they cannot pass over it" (Jer 5:22).

Last but not least, other fragments picture God as enthroned after the defeat of chaos and evil, reigning over it. One psalmist proclaims, "the LORD sits enthroned over the flood; the LORD sits enthroned as king forever" (Ps 29:10). The same image appears later in Judaism amongst the writings of the community that produced the Dead Sea Scrolls: "great and holy are you, YHWH, the Holy One of the holy ones from generation to generation. In front of him walks glory and behind him the roaring of many waters" (11Q5 26.9–10a).[34] God is seated in the throne room of heaven. The defeated chaos waters roar in the background whilst the glory of God fills the sanctuary.

Jews and early Christians clearly knew of a mythical tradition in which God battled the dragon and the sea but they used this myth differently. Other ancient Near Eastern traditions told the whole story. Biblical texts and other Jewish and Christian texts only use bits and pieces from the story. They obviously know the story but never tell it as a story in its own right. Scenes and snippets from the myth are always recounted in the context of another story, prayer, or hymn. Dragons may have snuck into Scripture but they seem to play a game of "now you see me, now you don't." What are they up to?

PLAYING WITH POETRY

The colorful storytelling of the Babylonian, Hittite, and Canaanite versions of the myth is missing in the Jewish and Christian versions of the myth. Part of this must be the effect of monotheism. Jews and Christians can hardly narrate the wrangling between the gods that occurs in the Babylonian or Ugaritic texts because they only acknowledged the existence of *one* God. However, this cannot be the whole reason. Around the turn of the eras, the Jewish community at Qumran were writing of a battle royal that would take place between the archangelic captain of God's heavenly host and the

---

34. The text 11Q5 can be found in the Dead Sea Scrolls.

denizens of demons led by prince of darkness.[35] Although we do not have complete versions of these stories, what we do possess suggests that some Jews were perfectly capable of writing myths with storylines that were as intricate as those of the ancient Near Eastern versions of the myth.

More likely Jewish and Christian tradition was not primarily interested in the story itself but the theological use that might be made of the story. If dragon stories were well known, then playing with the plot might make for a creative and effective way of making statements about God that would move people to belief in a way that bare statements about God have never really had the ability to do. Songs, poems, and stories convey much more powerfully and deeply religious truths than do (dry) doctrinal statements.

We see this in Psalm 104. The psalmist looks out to sea and tells the gathered worshippers "yonder is the sea, great and wide . . . there go the ships and Leviathan that you formed to sport in it" (Ps 104:25–26). The psalmist knows the story of the conquest of chaos. It has been told earlier in the psalm. God rides out in his cloud chariot (Ps 104:3–4) and defeats the waters of chaos, which flee in terror (Ps 104:7–9). Leviathan is the powerful dragon that alongside the sea threatens to engulf the world in chaos again. God's final speech in Job leaves the reader with no doubt that biblical tradition sees Leviathan as a wild, violent, and (apart from God) unconquerable monster (Job 41:1–34). However, the psalmist chooses to describe Leviathan as a plaything, a toy. God has created Leviathan as something to muck about in the sea.

This picture turns the normal story on its head. Firstly, God creates Leviathan. In the *Enuma Elish* (and possibly in other ancient Near Eastern myths) the warrior god struggles with the monster in order to overcome it. Unless it is defeated the forces of chaos will reign and creation will be impossible. As the psalmist has God create Leviathan, it is no longer the monster that pre-exists creation and that must be defeated for creation to happen. The words "which you formed" reduce Leviathan to one aspect of creation rather than the primordial force that stands against creation. They reduce Leviathan to a shadow of its former self. The idea that Leviathan is created to play around in the sea also adds a comical touch to this cosmic demotion.[36] Not only does Leviathan not threaten God as the dragon that

---

35. See the *War Scroll* and 11QMelchizedek. Both these texts may be found in the Dead Sea Scrolls.

36. Levenson, *Creation*, 17. One of his students suggests that Leviathan has become God's "rubber duckey"—a comment I find not only perceptive but also comforting as I realize that I am not the only person who was sufficiently irreverent as a student to draw

dwells in the primordial ocean before creation but Leviathan's sole reason for existence is play. Little could demean this mighty military monster further.

The relegation of Leviathan to the ranks of creatures God has created for amusement belittles the power of the monster. As the monster seems weaker than myths suggest, God appears correspondingly stronger. God must be stronger in order to be able to control such a beast with such ease. The psalmist plays with the story to make a theological point. Those who knew the story would get the point.

Like the Magi in the Christmas story, dragons came from the East. From their home territory in the myths of ancient Near Eastern cultures, they migrated into the faith, stories, and religious imagination of the biblical authors. From there it was just a few short steps into the biblical texts themselves. However, Jews and early Christians used the story differently from their Babylonian, Hittite, and Ugaritic counterparts. They do not seem to have been interested in it for its own sake. Rather, they ransacked the story for scenes and snippets that would suit their purposes. They wanted to tell it (or bits of it) in new and creative ways that would help them to understand God, their world, and their relationship with God better—and in particular, they used the story to picture how they lived with suffering and God.

---

this particular analogy.

2

FROM CHAOS TO CREATION
AND BACK AGAIN

THE STORIES WE TELL ourselves and each other shape our lives by shaping our expectations of ourselves and of the world around us. The way we picture our world and the possibilities it presents to us informs the way we choose to live.[1] The way we picture the world can have a positive or negative effect on the way we live. For some the world is alive with possibilities and opportunities. Others have a picture of the world that has nothing to offer and gives little, if any, freedom to choose how to live. We simply have to cope with the hand that life has dealt us. The stories we tell ourselves about the world shape the way we live.

Biblical authors did much the same thing with stories as did their contemporaries in other nations. The ancient Near Eastern stories of the divine warrior defeating chaos were used to shape peoples' expectations of life. They were used to encourage and to inspire. They were also used as tools to manipulate and oppress others, diminishing their self-respect and sense of self-worth at the same time as teaching them to expect little from life. The Babylonian version, the *Enuma Elish*, depicts the creation of the world with a message to the effect that Babylon was created as the center of the world to dominate all other nations. This is the way the world was created and this is the way the world should be. Certain biblical authors took this

---

1. A classic elaboration of this theme within social-scientific study is Berger and Luckmann, *Social Construction*.

Babylonian myth apart, shouting back that the world ought not to be like that. They used their biblical version of the myth to set up different expectations of life, that God would restore, favor, and prosper Israel despite their suffering at the hands of the Babylonians. Later writers in the biblical tradition asked questions of the biblical version of the myth, questioning how realistic it was and asking whether it might need revising so that it might come to terms with religious and political reality the way people actually experience it.

CHAOS, CRISIS, AND CREATION

Stories of creation often frame the way we see the world and our place within it. Where they involve divine beings of any kind, these stories also shape our understanding of our relationship with God or the gods. When the Babylonian warrior god Marduk conquers the monster Tiamat he creates the world out of her carcass (*Enuma Elish* IV 135—VI 10). After recovering from the fight Marduk splits the carcass of Tiamat in two and ensures that her chaos waters (her divided carcass) are guarded to prevent them coming together again (*Enuma Elish* IV 135–40):[2]

> He calmed down. Then the Lord was inspecting her carcass, that he might divide the monstrous lump and fashion artful things. He split her in two, like a fish for drying, half of her he set up as made as a cover, heaven. He stretched out the hide and assigned watchmen, and ordered them not to let her waters escape.

The escape of the waters would entail Tiamat coming together again. With this she would return and threaten the order of the gods and their world. Having curbed the threat, Marduk then creates the heavenly sanctuary in which the chief gods can dwell in luxury. Then he sets the stars in their place in heaven from where they can govern and order time. He makes special provision for the moon god and sun god as they have places of pre-eminence in governing time and the seasons. He gives them clear and detailed orders as to how they should relate to each other and order days and months. Marduk takes charge of the rain and mists himself and opens up underground springs from which the great Babylonian rivers, the Tigris and the Euphrates, flow. Whilst creating the waters he creates the

2. *COS* 1:398.

mountains, after which he forms the underworld. Then Marduk celebrates his newly won kingship with the gods and founds the city of Babylon.

This story celebrates the city of Babylon and glorifies the king of the gods of Babylon. It tells of how Babylon is safe from threat because its god has already faced the threat of chaos and death and has beaten these evils in battle. The establishment of the world out of the carcass of chaos and evil suggests that they are dead and life is assured. The guards who are ever watchful of the waters of Tiamat and keeping them within limits guarantee safety from catastrophe. Babylon not only has a special place in the world but in the heart of the only god who can defeat chaos and evil, assuring peace and security for all its citizens.[3] This story was dramatized every year at the annual *Akitu* festival where the Babylonians would celebrate their military strength and political domination over other nations.[4] This story and its yearly retelling was good news for Babylon.

The story may be heard very differently, however, if the audience comprises foreign captives. In the sixth century BC, the middle and ruling classes of Judah found themselves in exile in Babylon. They had once sung the songs of Zion, which told of how their God (the Lord Yahweh) had created Jerusalem similarly. It was founded on the waters of chaos and no enemy could assail it (e.g., Ps 46).[5] These songs now created a bitter taste in their mouths (see Ps 137).[6] They spoke of an inviolable city and temple but that city and its temple now lay devastated (see Ps 74; Lam 1–5).[7] The only songs of victory ringing in their ears would be those that were recited and sung at the Babylonian *Akitu* festival at which every year the *Enuma Elish* was recited and acted out. Marduk, his conquest of Tiamat, and the establishment of Babylon would have been celebrated before their eyes. The awful reality was that Babylon was established and Marduk to all intents and purposes appeared to have won the victory over all his enemies, including Judah and its god. The drama of the festival with its songs of celebration can have caused little but despondency amongst the Judean captives.

It was against this background that these captives were called to learn to sing again. A prophet arose and spoke of how God had finished

---

3. For a succinct introduction to the myth and its use, see Jacobsen, *Treasures*, 167–91.

4. Klein, "Akitu," 138–40.

5. Craigie, *Psalms 1–50*, 344–46.

6. Hossfeld and Zenger, *Psalms 3*, 514–16.

7. Hossfeld and Zenger, *Psalms 2*, 243–44; Hillers, *Lamentations*, 9–10.

punishing Judah for its sins. God was coming to rescue the people of Judah and return them to their own land (Isa 40:1–11). The prophet extolled God as creator of the universe (e.g., Isa 40:12–17) and as the one who conquered the chaos dragon (Isa 51:9–11).[8] The prophet tried to persuade the people that Marduk was a lifeless and powerless idol whose images would soon be carried in disgrace from Babylon, fleeing the Persian army as they took over the proud city of Babylon (Isa 44:9–20; 46:1–2).[9] The prophet was calling the people back to faith in God. It was easier to believe the *Enuma Elish*. It looked as if Marduk was the real conqueror of chaos and as if Marduk was the king of the universe but the prophet tried to persuade the people to believe a different story all the same.

Clearly some of the people of Judah in exile began to tell themselves a different story for this is when the famous creation account with which the Bible begins was most likely written. Telltale similarities between *Enuma Elish* and Genesis 1 have long suggested a relationship between them. The waters are split into two and placed above the heavens and below the earth. Marduk carves up Tiamat in this way. God divides the waters similarly (Gen 1:6–8). Both stories tell of the creation of the heavenly firmament, of dry land, of humanity, and of the sun, moon, and stars.[10] A brief comparison with the *Enuma Elish* suggests that Genesis 1:1—2:4a was written to inspire faith in God and suggest his power was greater than that of Babylon or its gods.[11]

Whereas the *Enuma Elish* begins with the creation of the gods, Genesis assumes that God has existed eternally. Marduk has to struggle against chaos in order to become king of the gods. God speaks and chaos (the formless and void of Gen 1:2) becomes what God wishes at nothing more than a word of command. The *Enuma Elish* takes time to explain the celestial settings of the Sun and Moon gods and explains their actions in great detail. Similar respect is shown to the star gods. By contrast Genesis does not even name the sun and moon, calling them the greater and lesser light

---

8. Baltzer, *Deutero-Isaiah*, 355–59. Blenkinsopp, *Isaiah 40–55*, 331–35.

9. Baltzer, *Deutero-Isaiah*, 190–204, 255–57. Blenkinsopp, *Isaiah 40–55*, 240–42; 267.

10. See the classic statements of this position in Gunkel (*Creation*, 78–111) and Heidel (*Babylonian Genesis*). For a revision of the original thesis but one that acknowledges the parallels, see the recent commentary Cotter (*Genesis*, 9–10). For recent restatements of the thesis, see Levenson (*Creation*, especially pp. 121–22), Batto ("Creation Theology," 32–38), and Moberly (*Theology*, 55–69).

11. Hasel ("Polemic Nature," 81–91). Similarly Wenham (*Genesis 1–15*, 9).

(Gen 1:14–16). The effect is to demote these heavenly lights to the realm of the created. God alone is God. The creation of the stars is mentioned as a mere afterthought, ". . . and the stars" (Gen 1:16d), brusquely dismissing the possibility of their being offered any respect as heavenly beings.[12] The author of Genesis states emphatically through their telling of this story that the gods of Babylon are no gods and only the God of Judah is God.

The author of Genesis 1 tells another story about God. Marduk had to struggle to defeat the monster Tiamat. Nowhere does God struggle against chaos in this Genesis creation story. Unlike Marduk, God is strong enough to conquer chaos with a word. However, dragons are not entirely absent from the Genesis creation story. They appear to be created alongside other sea creatures (Gen 1:21).[13] The text of Genesis 1 plays with the myth. God both creates out of chaos, the formless and void (Gen 1:2), and creates the chaos monsters (Gen 1:21). There is nothing odd about God destroying chaos and then creating chaos monsters because the author is playing with the myth like a poet using images to make a point. The author praises God as having the power to create out of chaos simply with a word, unlike the other so-called gods of the ancient Near East and particularly Marduk by whom the people of God have been fooled into thinking of themselves as valueless conquered slaves of a foreign power for too long. That is the message of creating out of chaos in verse 1. Our author calls the people of God to believe their lives have not dissolved into the chaos and evil of exile forever but that their God has complete control over the chaos monsters precisely because he created them. If God can create them by speaking a few words, he can surely destroy them equally easily. That is the message of God creating the monsters in verse 21. Both pictures say the same thing to the Jewish exiles: you may see yourselves as defeated forever but God has the power to conquer your chaos and create something beautiful for you instead. The author tries to inspire the Jewish exiles to understand that God has in mind a better future for them and that God has the power to bring this better future about.

This creation story (Gen 1:1—2:3) is a call to resilience. It speaks into the political suffering and humiliation of the defeated nation of Judah. They have heard the story of Marduk loudly and clearly and experienced

12. Hasel, "Polemic Nature," 88–89.

13. The Hebrew word *tannin* translates as dragon or sea monster. Wenham (*Genesis 1–15*, 24) suggests that the meaning of sea monster here may indicate the sovereignty of God over the forces of chaos.

the reality of Marduk in their daily lives in exile. However, the author of Genesis calls them to believe this story is a lie. The truth is God created the world, conquered chaos with more ease than Marduk could ever imagine, and has total control over chaos. The poet who penned this text asks the people of God to believe they can and will live out a different reality. The poet asks people to face their suffering with the faith that they belong in a different script, and that the God they worship can and will write the alternative script into being.

This new reality involves living a different quality of life and spirituality. God does not view people in the same way as Marduk. Marduk created human beings as slaves for the gods (*Enuma Elish* VI.7–9, 33–36).

> [Marduk said] "I shall make stand a human being, let 'Man' be its name. I shall create humankind. They shall bear the gods burden that those may rest. . . . From his [Qingu's] blood he made humankind. He imposed the burden of the gods and exempted the gods. After Ea the wise had made mankind, he imposed the burden of the gods on them!

The implication of the myth is clear enough. Human beings are of little value to the gods except for performing menial tasks of service that even the minor gods do not wish to perform. The Genesis creation story presents a totally different picture. Human beings are the pinnacle of creation. God makes humanity in the divine image and gives them dominion over the world. God entrusts creation to humanity, bestowing both great responsibility and dignity on people. Whereas Marduk treats people as slaves, God shows them the highest respect.[14] Those who follow the biblical God are to understand themselves as being people of value, dignity, and worth.

The creation story does not simply provide an ancient answer to the question of how we all got here, much as this is an important question. The myth seeks to provide the story by which God calls us to live. God calls people out of slavery and away from listening to and believing stories that we are to be enslaved to evil, injustice, and oppression. Instead God calls us to live lives full of the dignity and self-respect for which God created us originally. The story of our origins becomes the story of God's will for our destiny. It stands as a challenge to us, calling us to a life some of us find difficult to imagine. Yet there it stands beckoning us to walk in the way the biblical God sets before us.

14. Hasel, "Polemic Nature," 89–90.

WALKING IN THE WAY

The God of the Bible does not create humanity with dignity and worth so that these gifts can be thrown away in living life wastefully or foolishly. The rescue of the people of God from Babylon was not a political liberation that was to be followed by a moral free for all. The people arrived back in the land of Judah, repented of their sin, and committed themselves to live according to the commands of God (Neh 9–10).[15] Commitment to live out God's laws is the response love makes to God's action in saving us. It is also the only appropriate way of responding to rescue from sin and oppression as God gave these commands to ensure that people lived in ways that showed love and respect towards each other. This story of rescue, repentance, and committing to live according to the commands of God can be found elsewhere in the Bible.

This story also finds expression in the chaos myth. The first major section of the biblical book of Proverbs (Prov 1–9) comprises a speech from Wisdom, personified as a woman of great dignity and strength. Her speech counsels young men to live wisely. Towards the end of the speech she makes the following claim (Prov 8:22–31):

> The LORD created me at the beginning of his work, the first of his acts of long ago. Ages ago I was set up, at the first, before the beginning of the earth. When there were no depths I was brought forth, when there were no springs abounding with water. Before the mountains had been shaped, before the hills, I was brought forth—when he had not yet made earth and fields, or the world's first bits of soil. When he established the heavens, I was there, when he drew a circle on the face of the deep, when he made firm the skies above, when he established the fountains of the earth, then I was beside him like a master worker; and I was daily his delight, rejoicing before him always, rejoicing in his inhabited world, and delighting in the human race.

15. I am more than aware that the program of reform instituted by Ezra and Nehemiah does not sit easily with many contemporary or even New Testament ethical codes—particularly the divorcing of gentile wives (which contravenes the teaching of Jesus on divorce and shows a less inclusive attitude towards the gentiles than is found in Paul). However, the point I wish to make is that the reform of Ezra and Nehemiah was understood to be a response of covenant commitment to the covenant love of God, and the Torah was given as a gift for living life. I realize that this raises questions of ethics and personally I prefer the teachings of Jesus to many aspects of the Torah. I also realize that others do not. The questions this raises about what it means to follow the two great commands (love God and love your neighbor) are the subject of a separate discussion.

The text clearly refers to creation. The action of drawing a circle on the face of the deep is best compared to those texts that speak of God assigning limits to the chaos sea to prevent it from creating havoc (e.g., Job 38:8–11; Jer 5:22).[16] Creation involves controlling the chaos sea and preventing it from wreaking destruction. Wisdom is involved with God in this work of controlling the waters of chaos.

This poem about Wisdom's work in creation is embedded in her call to young men to follow her ways and not to walk in the paths of her opposite number, Lady Folly. Wisdom's basic message is that walking in the paths of, or living according to the precepts of, wisdom brings life, health, prosperity, and peace. Walking in the paths of folly brings poverty, devastation, and death. Embedding the creation poem within this speech underlines the basic idea that Wisdom is trying to convey. God and Wisdom created out of chaos, therefore the wise will live in ordered and stable ways. The wicked and foolish by their very actions undo creation for themselves and their universes dissolve back into chaos and death around them. Wisdom calls people to creation and life and away from the road to perdition.

Looking around at reality, some contemporary readers have wondered exactly how wise Wisdom could be as there are plenty of wicked people who thrive. Likewise there are good and honest people who do not seem to fare particularly well. By way of response to these questions, Michael Fox has suggested that the wisdom of Proverbs does not try to state how the world *is* but how the world *should be*. Wisdom works on the basis of a moral aesthetic that assumes there is coherence and harmony to the created order. Being wise entails acquiring "a sense of harmony, a sensitivity to what is fitting and right, in all realms of attitude and behaviour."[17] The wise have an appreciation of the fundamentally moral nature of the universe and of the morality required of human beings. From this starting point, the wise see that often the workings of the world and human society correspond to the harmony of Wisdom's vision. The wise also understand that the fundamentally moral nature of the universe is sometimes abrogated (e.g., Prov 10:15; 13:23; 14:20; 25:26). However, this outlook the wise have provides the basis for the prediction that the wicked, whilst they may prosper for a while, will receive the reward of their wickedness *in the end* (e.g., Prov 29:16). These

---

16. On Prov 8:22–31, see Murphy, *Proverbs*, 52. On Job 38:8–11, see Clines, *Job 38–42*, 1101–3. On Jer 5:22, see Lundbom, *Jeremiah 1–20*, 403. On all three texts, see Day, *God's Conflict*, 42–43, 56–57.

17. Fox, "Epistemology," 681.

predictions appear to be made on the basis of the moral aesthetic that lies at the heart of wisdom: that fundamentally things are good and that good will out in the end because God is good and has made all things good. The myth of Wisdom creating order out of chaos with God describes this moral aesthetic in picture form.

CRACKS IN THE CEILING OF HEAVEN

However, such a view may surely be challenged in the light of experience. The idea that people can live according to this moral aesthetic makes some sense when life is generally just and fair. Where undeserved suffering and injustice persist, the imagination of faith is increasingly stretched near its limits trying to read this harmony into lived reality. Hideous evils that continue unchecked present great challenges to this kind of thinking.

Greg Boyd tells the story of Zosia, a young girl whose eyes are plucked out by Nazi soldiers as her mother looks on in agony. Boyd makes the point that any theology that speaks of ultimate harmony in the universe is surely challenged by events like these.[18] He goes on to suggest that the biblical mythology of the struggle of the divine warrior against the powers of chaos provides a helpful theological model for coming to terms with suffering. Rather than trying to see the goodness of God in hideous evils, the faithful need to note that the Bible depicts God as creating out of chaos in the beginning and finally defeating all chaos and evil at the end.[19] Boyd recommends foregoing some traditional ideas of God being in control of reality in the meantime in favor of the idea that the forces of chaos (pictured in myth as Leviathan, Rahab, and the sea) sometimes rage and that God battles against them. He argues that whilst losing the idea of God in control may be scary for people of faith, "it certainly seems less scary than living in a cosmos that is being coercively run by a supreme being who secretly wills the torture of little girls."[20] His point is forcefully made.

Certainly the language of creation out of chaos can accommodate the realities of suffering. Leviathan, Rahab and her demonic hordes, and the chaos sea and rivers personify all that is evil and destructive of life, health, and prosperity. The depiction of these monsters ravaging creation in biblical poetry puts into picture form the belief that terrible evils occur. Moreover,

18. Boyd, *God at War*, 31–72.
19. Ibid., 73–113, 162–67.
20. Ibid., 292.

the biblical authors developed their use of the myth to give expression to the awfulness of suffering in its more extreme forms. Probably the clearest example of this is found in Daniel's vision of the four beasts (Dan 7:2–8):

> I, Daniel, saw in my vision by night the four winds of heaven stirring up the great sea, and four great beasts came up out of the sea, different from one another. The first was like a lion and had eagles' wings. Then, as I watched, its wings were plucked off, and it was lifted up from the ground and made to stand on two feet like a human being; and a human mind was given to it. Another beast appeared, a second one, that looked like a bear. It was raised up on one side, had three tusks in its mouth among its teeth and was told, "Arise, devour many bodies!" After this, as I watched, another appeared, like a leopard. The beast had four wings of a bird on its back and four heads; and dominion was given to it. After this I saw in the visions by night a fourth beast, terrifying and dreadful and exceedingly strong. It had great iron teeth and was devouring, breaking in pieces, and stamping what was left with its feet. It was different from all the beasts that preceded it, and it had ten horns. I was considering the horns, when another horn appeared, a little one coming up among them; to make room for it, three of the earlier horns were plucked up by the roots. There were eyes like human eyes in this horn, and a mouth speaking arrogantly.

This text develops the opening scene of the old biblical myth of God battling the sea and its chaos monsters. Rather than simply have Leviathan or Rahab in the sea, the author depicts four beasts arising from the sea. Their rising from the sea identifies them as chaos monsters.[21] Although the exact reasons for their strange depiction are not fully understood by scholars, their nature as mixed animals indicates that something is wrong. The Genesis creation story has God create by dividing and ordering—creation is fundamentally ordered. The fact that these beasts are made up of the body parts of various different animals and birds suggests that what they represent is fundamentally disordered. Creation has been undone.

The fourth beast is the exception to this rule. We have no access to what it might have looked like. At this point, the vision zooms in on its actions and we are given a picture of destruction. We catch glimpses of those parts of the beast that are wreaking this havoc, its teeth and its feet, almost like a camera capturing details of a wider canvas close up. The effect of focusing our attention on its great iron (unnatural, distortion of creation again) teeth

---

21. Collins, *Daniel*, 280–95.

and feet as they tear (presumably) God's people apart is to pull us into the danger zone and so fill us with the full horror of what is happening.

There was good reason for developing the myth in the direction of the horror movie genre. The book of Daniel was completed around the time of the persecution of the Jews by the Seleucid king Antiochus IV Epiphanes (represented in Daniel 7 by the arrogant horn of the fourth beast).[22] This was a time of horrendous suffering. The story of 2 Maccabees 7 relates the torture and death of seven brothers who, in defiance of Antiochus, refused to break the Torah by eating the flesh of swine. The first had his hands and feet cut off and his tongue cut out as his mother and brothers looked on, before being fried alive. They tore the hair and skin from the head of the second before killing him as they had his elder brother. The other brothers died similar and worse deaths before the mother, who having witnessed the torture of all her sons, also died.[23]

The events behind these martyrdom accounts constituted some of the realities through which the people to whom the book of Daniel was addressed were living. The horrors that some of them may have witnessed and about which many will have heard were given some kind of pictorial representation in the myth. The vision of the beasts coming out of the sea provided a religious language within which they could despair. To this extent, Greg Boyd makes a valid point. Creation has been undone. Mixed beasts rule and reality has become distorted. No longer does it bear the image or glory of its good creator but it is ripped apart by destructive monsters according to their rage and whim.

Nonetheless, the authors of these texts assume that God is in control.[24] Daniel speaks of the beasts in the passive, e.g., "its wings were plucked off and it was made to stand on two feet . . . and a human mind was given to it" (Dan 7:4). The second beast was raised up and told to devour (Dan 7:5). The third beast was given dominion (Dan 7:6). The reason for describing what happened in this way (sometimes called "the divine passive") is that the author assumes that God is in ultimate control. The vision of this control is lost in the depiction of the fourth beast, which speaks arrogantly against

22. Collins, *Daniel*, 61. For the identification of Antiochus IV Epiphanes as the fourth beast, see Collins, *Daniel*, 299.

23. 2 Maccabees may be found in the Apocrypha. For discussion of this text, its rhetorical goals and its historicity, see Doran, *2 Maccabees*, 1–13, 155–66.

24. Difficult though this is for many modern ears, the author of 2 Maccabees reads the suffering as being about the discipline of the people of Judah (Doran, *2 Maccabees*, 164).

God (Dan 7:7–8). However, to assume that ultimate control of reality has been wrested from God by the fourth beast would misrepresent the text as the following scene demonstrates (Dan 7:9–14):

> As I watched, thrones were set in place, and an Ancient One took his throne, his clothing was white as snow, and the hair of his head like pure wool; his throne was fiery flames, and its wheels were burning fire. A stream of fire issued and flowed out from his presence. A thousand thousands served him, and ten thousand times ten thousand stood attending him. The court sat in judgment, and the books were opened. I watched then because of the noise of the arrogant words that the horn was speaking. And as I watched, the beast was put to death, and its body destroyed and given over to be burned with fire. As for the rest of the beasts, their dominion was taken away, but their lives were prolonged for a season and a time. As I watched in the night visions, I saw one like a human being coming with the clouds of heaven. And he came to the Ancient One and was presented before him. To him was given dominion and glory and kingship, that all peoples, nations, and languages should serve him. His dominion is an everlasting dominion that shall not pass away, and his kingship is one that shall never be destroyed.

The fourth beast rages for a while but the court of heaven convenes and judges it and all the beasts.[25] The first three are imprisoned and the fourth is killed and burned. There may be a certain macabre irony in the mythical representation of Antiochus receiving a punishment not dissimilar from that which he meted out on faithful Jews. However, with the death of the fourth beast chaos is conquered and creation restored once again. The vision promotes the idea that God will intervene and restore creation and so does not lose sight of the idea that God is ultimately in control.

The myth tells two stories we can find difficult to reconcile theologically. It tells the story that God knows what is happening and behind the scenes is ultimately in control. God does not let the powers that be (for all that they cause suffering) get out of control. The myth speaks of God permitting or allowing suffering to happen. Even when the monsters seem to have the upper hand and events seem completely outside divine control (as with the activities of the fourth beast) the writer does not give up hope. The story states that at the end of time God will intervene and restore order. The fact that this story was most likely written during the period of suffering

---

25. Collins, *Daniel*, 303.

persecution under Antiochus IV Epiphanes bears striking witness to the faith of its author—this was no armchair exercise in philosophical theology.[26] The author told the story of God being in control from a situation of hopeless suffering.

However, the myth also tells the story of the horror and violence of evil. There is no attempt to veil the destruction that the fourth beast wreaks. Physical destruction is an interesting metaphor for the author to use. Antiochus IV Epiphanes built a gymnasium in Jerusalem and attempted to bring the benefits of Greek culture to his Jewish audience (1 Macc 1:12–14). Outwardly, Antiochus was constructive. Unlike the Babylonians before him, he did not destroy the temple—he simply tried to bring multi-cultural worship into this holy space by constructing an altar to his own god, Zeus, on the altar of the holiest place in the Jerusalem temple.[27] However, what seemed to Antiochus to be the triumph of civilization was to faithful Jews the destruction of their religious world. The metaphor of physical destruction wrought by the fourth beast describes what outwardly might look like the development of culture. This picture of the fourth beast captures the destruction of the religious world that Antiochus' attempt to spread Greek culture involved. As well as describing this, it depicts dismemberment of individuals who had the courage to resist the tearing apart of their religious world. The violent language captures the realities of both physical and religious violence suffered by those to whom the vision of Daniel 7 is addressed. No attempt is made to soften the violence.

Like many who write on this text today, I sit in an armchair typing at a computer in a largely democratic nation that is wealthier than most others, making my relative situation in life quite comfortable. I probably need to listen to the voices of those who have spoken from the kind of suffering that those who wrote Daniel from their situation under Antiochus have undergone. The testimony that has come down to us from those who suffered under Antiochus was to hold both to telling the story of present suffering in all its pain and horror, and to tell the story of God in control.

Such storytelling rarely pleases those who want try to explain life, including suffering, rationally and logically. There are implied contradictions. God cannot be faithful to the people of God and permit this kind of suffering. However, this storytelling does not raise these contradictions

26. For the argument for the date of Daniel 7 as taking place during the persecution under Antiochus, see Collins, *Daniel*, 324.

27. Ibid., 357–58.

as issues. The pain is felt and the story tells it. There is no avoidance of the issues. However, the story that God is in control and will rescue is told in hope that it will come true again. The biblical myth tells both the story of suffering and the story of salvation.

I am going to hazard the suggestion that this is an advantage biblical myth holds over much philosophical and theological thought. The myth does not attempt to reconcile the tensions in the present. It does not add to present suffering the spiritual indignity of divesting people of the right to believe because they cannot solve the theological conundrum of evil. Faith, however naive in the face of present evils, is assumed and encouraged—faith in the presence of God, even when God seems absent; as well as faith that God will someday somehow rescue the faithful. However, this faith is not required to believe against all experience that the suffering of the persecuted faithful is anything other than unbearable, wrong, and completely against the will of God. Indeed, the embodiment of their suffering as chaos monsters expresses precisely that such suffering is all of these things.

The myth provides space in which to locate oneself theologically and spiritually. Rather than trying to explain reality in a neat and logical argument, the myth offers a very basic storyline with different elements (the raging of the monsters, the judgment of God, the destruction of the monsters) that hold all the different experiences of those suffering under Antiochus IV Epiphanes within its imagery and plot. The story does not shirk from recognizing suffering but evil does not have the last word. The different elements of the plot provide space for exploration of present suffering and hope for the future. This plot allows for all the tensions of the lived realities to be embraced by the faithful. The imagery gives scope for exploring and expressing the violence and horror of present suffering in ways that give vent to emotions. In retelling the story, the faithful are enabled to bring their realities before God however present or absent God seems or feels.

WHEN CRACKS BECOME CHASMS

Sometimes, and for some people, theology breaks down under the weight of experience. The faithful disagree over the faithfulness of God. People ask questions of the scriptural story and wonder whether the story might be told in ways more true to experience. This is nothing new. The very same questions can be heard in the disagreements over dragons. Were they conquered at creation? Or did God merely tame them, and if so, how long did the effects last? Do we live in a precarious world where chaos might unleash its devastating power at any moment? Did God ever gain control over evil or is it simply built into the universe?

Canonical Scripture places the creation story of Genesis 1:1—2:3 at the beginning. In occupying this place of pre-eminence it inevitably casts its light (or shadow) over what follows and to a certain extent provides the framework within which what follows is read. In terms of our myth of the conquest of chaos, it suggests the complete control of God over evil and denies the idea that chaos is an independent reality that co-existed alongside God before creation. The Genesis creation story brooks no rivals, for God does not allow for anything in reality to ultimately be outside God's control.

However, there lurk within biblical writings stories of God's battle with the forces of chaos in which the creation of the world seems to follow the conquest of chaos (e.g., Pss 74:12–17; 89:8–12). The effect of putting Genesis 1:1—2:3 at the head of the biblical narrative has been to make its reading of creation normative. The idea of God fighting monsters prior to creation becomes a minor variation on the theme of God creating out of chaos effortlessly and without need of a battle.

On occasion the variation becomes the theme. One such may be found in the deuterocanonical book of *4 Ezra*.[28] The author is meditating on the (un)faithfulness of God in the wake of the Roman destruction of Jerusalem in AD 70.[29] The temple has been destroyed. The nation has been humiliated by a foreign power. Its leaders have been taken into exile and killed. The promises of salvation and renewed political freedom from the foreign oppressor have been smashed to pieces in the light of recent events. The author of *4 Ezra* rehearses the creation story in one of his prayers in which he seeks to discover what God is doing and why God does not seem to be faithful to the covenant. The story of the creation of sea creatures on the fifth day is told in the following manner (*4 Ezra* 6:49–52):

> Then you kept in existence two living creatures; the one you called
> Behemoth and the name of the other Leviathan. And you sepa-
> rated one from the other, for the seventh part where the water had
> been gathered together could not hold them both. And you gave
> Behemoth one of the parts that had been dried up on the third
> day, to live in it, where there are a thousand mountains; but to

28. *4 Ezra* may be found in the Apocrypha.

29. Many Jews of this period had expected God to conquer Rome rather than to have Rome defeat them, destroy their holy city, and exile the leaders of the nation.

> Leviathan you gave the seventh part, the watery part; and you have
> kept them to be eaten by whom you wish, and when you wish.

Leviathan and Behemoth are two chaos monsters. Leviathan appears in various biblical texts as the enemy of God (e.g., Ps 74:13–14; Isa 27:1). Behemoth only appears in Job 40:15–24. The author of 4 Ezra replaces the great sea monsters of Genesis 1:21 with a reference to Leviathan and Behemoth.[30]

This retelling of the story is theologically slightly subversive. Rather than choosing to follow the main story of God being so powerful that even the chaos monsters would not exist had God not created them, the author follows the variation on the theme and places it in the center of the creation story. The beasts are kept alive at creation, they are not destroyed. They are given allotted realms in which to dwell. God's control over them is still celebrated as they are kept in existence to be eaten at the end of time when God destroys all chaos and evil (compare the vision in 2 Baruch 29:4).[31] However, God has not created them nor has he destroyed them. The monsters have existence independent of God before creation and represent powers opposing God that God has not fully subdued. The author seems to want creation to reflect their reality of chaos and suffering, and so they adjust the story of creation accordingly leaving the dragons in existence ready to rear their ugly heads at any moment.

Interestingly some versions of 4 Ezra 6:49 add the words "two living creatures, *which you had created*," while others omit them.[32] The original text of 4 Ezra is probably impossible to recover from the versions we possess and so it is difficult to reconstruct the original reading of this verse with any certainty.[33] Nonetheless, the two different versions of this text look suspiciously like an early argument over the sovereignty of God. One version suggests that there were chaos monsters before God created and that God did not fully eliminate them or subdue them but kept them in creation. This suggests that there is an element of chaos in reality that God might never have had fully under control. The other version, which adds

---

30. Stone, 4 Ezra, 186.

31. Ibid., 186–87. The book of 2 Baruch may be found in the Pseudepigrapha.

32. Ibid., 179. Many ancient texts survive in a number of different versions. Scholars try to work out which of these versions is the most original when they translate and publish these texts for us to read. Working out the original version can be a very complex process and sometimes we simply cannot be certain what the original text really was.

33. Ibid., 8–9.

"which you had created," suggests that God originally created the monsters and then kept them in existence when creating the rest of the world. This reading ensures that the existence of the chaos monsters does not imply anything is outside of God's control and so preserves the power of God over evil. These early authors and editors seem to be grappling with and arguing over the possibility that God might not be quite so in control after all. The debate that Boyd and others are having today over how far we can say God really is in control of the chaos we see around us was known and had in the ancient world as well.

Some in the ancient world were keener to preserve the omnipotence of God. The author of *Jubilees*, a Jewish text from the second century BC, resolves the same difference in the texts in the following way (*Jub.* 2:11): "And on the fifth day he created the great sea monsters in the midst of the depths of the waters—for these were made by his hands as the first corporeal beings."[34] This creation account has no hint of creation out of chaos let alone divine battle before creation (2:2–16). The chaos monsters are most definitely one of the acts of God in creation and their preceding all other creatures in the order of creation may have been an attempt to go some way towards reconciling the differences between biblical texts, which have the monsters created, and other texts, which have them exist before creation.

Whatever the retellings of individual writers, the Genesis creation story gave a very positive spin on the control God has over the powers of evil and chaos. In its own era and down the ages, it offers a powerful message of a God who cares, comes to rescue, and who calls us to lead lives of self-respect, mutual respect, and freedom. However, the myth on which it draws is malleable and at the fringes of the canonical story; other authors have been minded, in the face of their own experience, to ask whether the authors of Genesis were not a little over-optimistic in their presentation of the faith. The malleability of the story may open it up to distortion from the perspective of those of us who hold to a particular version of religious orthodoxy. However, it is also the genius of the myth.

The story is not fixed. It has boundaries in that there is a plot. Generally this moves from chaos to creation, although sometimes it moves from creation to chaos and back to creation again. However, within the overall outline there is room for improvisation. Our lives are all different and so the story invites us to shape it in order to help us sing of our own experiences. No two dragons are the same. Some are dead, some are subdued, and

34. *OTP* 2:56.

others are very much alive and kicking. We are invited not only to sketch but also to color in our own dragons so that they reflect our own sufferings and challenges. The myth can be molded to fit our realities and yet the expectation is that the story will finally break the mold when suffering is past and difficulties are resolved.

The invitation is to participate faithfully in the story and its expectations. From the beginning, the creation story has offered a vision of a better world and a God who is determined to bring this into being. As hearers of the story, we are asked to let go our other stories that tell of anything less than lives and communities full of worth and creativity. We are called into greater love for others and for ourselves, and to live in ways that embody this love and respect in just and generous living. We are given the space to recognize that life is not always like this and a language in which to picture the worst at the same time as holding out hope—and it is to exploring how this language works in prayer we now turn.

3

OUT OF THE DEPTHS

THE BEST STORYTELLERS ARE not necessarily those who can spin a yarn or those who have the gift of the gab. There is something quite compelling about listening to a story—however simply or disjointedly told—by someone who has lived or currently lives the story. Authenticity breaks through in a way that is very difficult to capture in any kind of imitation of reality or variation on a theme from experience. Many of the prayers we find in the psalms of Israel are cries from and meditations on personal experience. The psalmists tell their stories vividly, with an authenticity that is surely part of the reason that generations of people from various religious traditions and from none have found solace and inspiration in their words down the ages. Sometimes they tell their stories from the thick of the experience. Other times they tell the stories from the distance of thoughtful reflection. Frequently their storytelling resonates across the time and cultural gaps between their worlds and ours.

Some of the more gripping moments in the psalms may be found in the laments, where the psalmists pour out a welter of thoughts and reactions in what can come across as a torrent of emotion. These laments are sometimes spoken on behalf of the whole community, summing up the experience and feelings of the community and placing before God their agonizing questions and their inmost longings. Other times these laments are quite personal and concern the lives and sufferings of individuals. These are psalms of many colors, textures, and tones that open up a world in which contemporary people of faith are able to find words to express their own experience or to help them find the words they need themselves to say and pray.

Some of the psalms draw on the language of the divine warrior conquering the forces of chaos. Commenting on these psalms, Jon Levenson notes how the psalmists use this language to bring their suffering before God. The psalmists take or write hymns glorifying God conquering chaos and insert them into psalms that describe the horrendous suffering of God's people. In the face of their suffering, they do not abandon the text of the myth as hollow liturgy that has no power to speak into present reality. Instead they embrace the old story as speaking of the true nature of the God they worship. So they use the hymns to rebuke God and cajole God into action. Remembering his past acts of destroying chaos reminds God that there is contemporary chaos that needs to be subdued. The psalmists do not promote smug faith, openly acknowledging that God has not acted to save when that is the case. Neither do they assume that evil has triumphed or can do so. The very act of cajoling God into action assumes that God has power over chaos. The ritual act of lament becomes the place where the psalmists reconcile the reality of suffering with their belief in the faithfulness, power, and goodness of God.[1] Where modern theologians often seek explanations for suffering, their ancient counterparts turned instead to prayer.

It cannot be doubted that the ancients used the story of God conquering dragons in prayers that offered ritual space to come to terms with suffering. The evidence that Levenson reviews, particularly in Psalm 74 and Isaiah 51, strongly supports his analysis.[2] However, not all texts cajole God into renewed acts of creation out of chaos. The psalmists react to suffering in a variety of ways and their use of the dragon myth reflects some of these. Below we will explore four different ways in which psalmists prayed through the myth in order to help them come to terms with their experiences of suffering.

PSALM 74: LOOKING FORWARD IN ANGER

Psalm 74 reflects the situation of those left in the land when the leaders of the nation of Judah were carried off into exile in Babylon in the sixth century BC. The book of Lamentations offers a gut-wrenching picture of the devastation of Jerusalem. Rape, starvation, and torture are overlaid by

1. Levenson, *Creation*, 17–25.
2. Ibid., 17–21.

national humiliation (Lam 2:1–2; 5:1–12). In terms of trying to work out where God is in all of this, the book moves from speaking of the anger of God (Lam 1:12–18) with terror at the violence of God's judgment (Lam 2:1–8), through a sense of reconciliation to the discipline of God (Lam 3:19–33), to a sense of abandonment by God accompanied by a desperate plea that God might heal and restore (Lam 5:19–22).[3] This devastation and these reactions to it offer us insights into the religious, political, and human situation from which Psalm 74 was written and spoken.

Psalm 74 opens with a direct accusation. The psalmist asks why God has abandoned the covenant people (Ps 74:1–2). They invite God on a guided tour of the temple in Jerusalem, stopping to view its ruins and describe in intricate detail the events that led to its destruction (Ps 74:3–8). They follow this with a direct address in which they ask exactly how long God intends to allow this situation to continue (Ps 74:9–11). Before moving on to demand that God remembers the covenant, rescues the people and attends to the victory shouts of their enemies, the psalmist sings the following hymn (Ps 74:13–17):[4]

> You divided the sea by your might; you broke the heads of the dragons in the waters. You crushed the heads of Leviathan; you gave him as food for the creatures of the wilderness. You cut openings for springs and torrents; you dried up ever-flowing streams. Yours is the day, yours also the night; you established the luminaries and the sun. You have fixed all the bounds of the earth; you made summer and winter.

The psalmist bursts into praise of God. God divided the sea and destroyed Leviathan. God conquered chaos and created the world. The cutting open of the earth for springs and torrents may reflect the kind of scene we find in the *Enuma Elish* where Marduk creates holes in the carcass of Tiamat for the waters to flow through in a controlled and life-giving manner (*Enuma Elish* V 50–56).[5] God dried up the chaos waters and in doing so defeated

---

3. Hillers, *Lamentations*, 3–6.

4. For an analysis of the structure of Psalm 74, see Hossfeld and Zenger, *Psalms 2*, 241–42.

5. Emerton ("Spring," 122–33) argues that the cutting open of springs and torrents is to drain the chaos waters away on the basis that the drying up of the ever-flowing streams that follows assumes this. However, one might equally easily read an interlocking structure in this creation out of chaos hymn. Chaos is defeated in verses 12–14, creation begins in verse 15a, chaos is defeated in verse 15b, and creation is finished in verses 16–17. On either reading the text refers to the defeat of chaos.

them. Then God completes creation, fixing everything in its proper order (Ps 74:16–17).

The contrast between the orderliness of creation and the chaos of the ruined temple could not be starker or more deliberate. The irony could not be more vicious. The psalmist takes God on a tour of the destruction of the temple (Ps 74:3–8). Standing in its ruins, they point out the absence of prophetic ministry in the temple (Ps 74:9).[6] The psalmist then stands there, surrounded by destruction, and sings a hymn in praise of the mighty acts of the God who destroys chaos and creates order. It is unlikely that the psalmist is suddenly moved from despair to praise because immediately after the hymn of praise comes this accusation: "Remember this, O LORD, how the enemy scoffs, and an impious people reviles your name" (Ps 74:18). Rather the psalmist performs a remarkably pointed act of protest.

The temple was the meeting place of heaven and earth. Just as God sat enthroned above the subdued waters of chaos in heaven (Ps 104:3a), so God dwelt in the temple on earth. The temple represented God's mastery over the universe and God's gracious rule over the covenant people. During festivals in the temple, the covenant people would recite psalms celebrating God's victory over chaos and gift of peace and prosperity to the people.[7]

Now the temple lies in ruins. The people are conquered and their leaders are in exile in Babylon. Peace and prosperity have been replaced by political domination and the aftermath of violent invasion. The psalmist stands amongst the ruins and sings a song of the LORD of Zion who had conquered chaos and created order. Sitting in between rebukes the psalmist fires off at God, the hymn takes on an angry, almost sarcastic tone.

But there is faith in these rebukes. The psalmist asks God how long this situation will continue (Ps 74:10). They assume that God can do something about the situation, accusing God of choosing not to act (Ps 74:11). They cajole God into action, noting that their enemies insult God (Ps 74:18). They call on God to rise up and persuade the court of heaven that it is time

---

6. Hossfeld and Zenger, *Psalms 2*, 245; Kraus, *Psalms 60–150*, 99; Tate, *Psalms 50–100*, 249.

7. Reconstructions of exactly what kinds of psalms were sung at exactly what sort of festival in pre-exilic Israel remains a matter of some debate. For the classic and controversial thesis, see Mowinckel *The Psalms*. For a cautious assessment of the issue, affirming the nature of cultic psalms as being composed for festival liturgies whilst noting the paucity of data we have for reconstructing the nature of such festival liturgies, see Kraus, *Psalms 1–50*, 56–66. For a more recent reconstruction of the festival, see Croft, *Identity*, 80–113, 131–32.

to reverse the situation on earth (Ps 74:22). The psalmist knows that God can act and tries to persuade God to act.

The chaos myth is used here to rebuke God and persuade God into action, much as Levenson suggests. However, the mimicry of temple worship in a situation that is as s far cry from the vision of the songs of worship is not simply angry. It is also quite pathetic. The psalmist cannot sing the songs of Zion in the heart of Jerusalem without their seeming laughably inappropriate. The beliefs to which they bear witness could not be further from the present reality. The scene of the psalmist singing the song can only evoke sympathy.

There is something quite powerful about the way in which the psalmist sings of God's conquest over chaos. At one and the same time, this song embodies both the despair and the faith of the psalmist. The scene itself highlights the reason for despair: given the contemporary situation of Jerusalem, there simply was no reason to praise God for eliminating evil. However, the myth speaks of a God who will do these things and so, from anger and despair, the psalmist cries out in fragile faith for God to rise up and take action.

PSALM 89: A CASE OF DOUBLE IRONY

This is a beautifully crafted psalm, dividing roughly into three sections, each with its own distinct style.[8] The opening section is a hymn of praise, glorifying the LORD God of hosts for mighty acts in creation and for faithfulness towards the covenant people (Ps 89:1–18). A psalm of gratitude for the covenant God made with King David follows in the second section, celebrating the special relationship God has with the covenant people (Ps 89:19–37). This is followed rather suddenly and unexpectedly by a very bitter lament about the actual situation of the psalmist (assumed to be the king, a descendant of David), that he has been defeated in battle and the enemies of the covenant people triumph.[9]

8. In what follows I follow the standard reading that verse 52 is really the ending of the third book of the psalms and did not originally belong to Psalm 89, which ends with the stinging rebuke of verse 51. For details, see Hossfeld and Zenger, *Psalms 2*, 413. Further subdivisions might be made that place verses 1–2 with verses 5–18, and verses 3–4 with verses 19–37. For the purposes of the overall reading here, this makes little difference.

9. These sections within the psalm are so distinct that some scholars reckon that the psalm is composite. Different sections were composed at different times before the

The psalmist celebrates the steadfast love and faithfulness of God, extolling both twice in the opening verses and underlining that they last forever (Ps 89:1–2). Having established this as their theme, the psalmist begins a crescendo of praise. They extol the faithfulness (Ps 89:5, 8, 14) and steadfast love of God (Ps 89:14) with respect to God ruling heaven and earth, establishing righteousness and justice. Of particular interest is the way in which God's conquest of chaos appears as an example of God's faithfulness (Ps 89:8–11):

> O LORD God of hosts, who is as mighty as you, O LORD? Your faithfulness surrounds you. You rule the raging of the sea; when its waves rise, you still them. You crushed Rahab like a carcass; you scattered your enemies with your mighty arm. The heavens are yours, the earth also is yours; the world and all that is in it—you have founded them.

Rahab the chaos monster has been slain and God's enemies are conquered. The raging chaos sea has been quieted. God is in control of evil and suffering and in this demonstrates faithfulness to the covenant people. As if to underline the point further, the psalmist introduces the theme of the covenant that God made with David (Ps 89:3).

In the following section, the psalmist takes the praise to an even higher plane. God has promised faithfulness to the king of the covenant people eternally and proclaims that this is no lie (Ps 89:35–6). The use of the key words continues to bolster the impression of the everlasting commitment of God to the covenant people. God promises that the covenant will remain firm forever (Ps 89:28, 34). God promises to show David faithfulness and steadfast love unwaveringly (Ps 89:24, 28, 33). Again the psalmist links this to mastery over the forces of chaos, only this time God demonstrates faithfulness and steadfast love by giving David control over chaos (Ps 89:24–5):

> My faithfulness and steadfast love shall be with him; and in my name his horn shall be exalted. I will set his hand on the sea and his right hand on the rivers.

---

whole psalm was put together in its present form (Hossfeld and Zenger, *Psalms 2*, 402; Tate, *Psalms 51–100*, 413–14). On the other hand, there are various key words that recur throughout the psalm, giving the sense that it ought to be read as a whole and so providing some evidence that it might have been composed as a unity originally (Goldingay, *Psalms 2*, 664–65). Whatever the answer to this question, in its present form the psalm works on account of the way in which its key words tie together three different kinds of psalm in each of the three sections.

The pairing of sea and rivers refers to the waters of chaos (Nah 1:4; Hab 3:8) and probably reflects the same pairing in the Ugaritic myth of Ba'lu and Yammu (e.g., *KTU* 1.2 i 41).[10] The cash value of this promise of mastery over chaos appears to be victory over his enemies and peace and security in the nation (Ps 89:22–23, 27).

But nothing could seem further from the truth to the psalmist. The promises to David appear to have been systematically overturned. God anointed David (Ps 89:20) but has now rejected his anointed towards whom God shows only wrath (Ps 89:38). God established a covenant with David (Ps 89:28, 34), which God has now renounced (Ps 89:39). God promised that David would defeat his enemies (Ps 89:22–23), yet the king lies defeated at the hands of his enemies (Ps 89:43). God set David's right hand over all chaos (Ps 89:25), yet it is the right hand of the king's enemies that God has exalted (Ps 89:42). God set a crown on David (Ps 89:19), yet has removed the scepter from the hand of the king and has hurled his throne to the ground (Ps 89:44). God has not made good on any of the promises to David.

The psalm seethes with frustration and anger. The psalmist has quoted God referring to David as "my servant" in the first two sections (Ps 89:3, 20). Now they hurl the commitment back at God, asking why God has renounced the covenant with "your servant" and cajoling God into silencing those who taunt "your servant" (Ps 89:39, 50). The bitterness of the psalm finds its full flourishing in the final verses. Having outlined how God has failed to keep the promises to the Davidic king, the psalmist asks God where the promised faithfulness and steadfast love actually are, sardonically echoing the opening praises of the psalm (Ps 89:49).

The psalmist leads the worshipper on a journey. Praise for God's mastery over creation overflows into extolling the covenant that God swore to David. The celebration of God's faithfulness to the people of the covenant reaches dizzying heights before the psalmist brings it crashing to earth in the face of reality. Looking back over the psalm, the worshipper realizes that the praise has been at best ironic. The psalmist has not been celebrating God's mastery over chaos but has been complaining bitterly of the victory of a revitalized Rahab over the covenant people.

---

10. Hossfeld and Zenger, *Psalms 2*, 410; Tate, *Psalms 51–100*, 423.

Reflections Then and Now

Angry and bitter lament has become fashionable in some quarters. React-ing against dry theology that analyzes texts to the point where they lose all power, some would encourage us to re-enter the poetry of biblical lament and allow ourselves to feel the force of the language. They invite us to relate our own reactions in the face of (perceived) injustices to those of the psalm-ists. In the face of a practice of faith that can become facile in its failure to recognize suffering, they are reaffirming lament as a language people of faith need to re-learn if they are to live authentic lives as worshippers of the true and living God. This redressing of the balance seems quite wholesome.

However, it is not without its own dangers. Lament can bring back into faith and worship an important dimension that has been missing in some forms of contemporary worship and spirituality. Nonetheless, it might also run the risk of becoming a new narcissism. Without the balance provided by spiritual practices like *examen* through which we ask ourselves what we have done wrong and which enable us to see both the discipline and chastisement of God in our lives, lament can become the adolescent cries of undisciplined children who are screaming because their perceived needs have not been fulfilled in the desired manner and within the desired timescale.

There can be little doubt that the biblical God sends chaos and suf-fering as judgment on we who sin. Isaiah 8:7 compares the king of Assyria to the waters of chaos God sends in punishment on the sinful covenant people.[11] The story of Noah uses the myth in the same way but referring to God's judgment on the whole world. In creation the chaos waters are split, with half placed above the heavens and half placed below the earth (Gen 1:6–8). When humanity sins sufficiently, God opens up the fountains of the great deep and lets the chaos waters flood through onto the earth. At the same time God allows the chaos waters to pour out through the windows of heaven (Gen 7:11).[12] God brings the waters of chaos from above the heav-ens and below the earth to flood the earth in punishment for the sins of humanity.[13] God uses chaos to judge sinful humanity.

11. Day, *God's Conflict*, 103–4 ; Blenkinsopp, *Isaiah 1–39*, 240.

12. Wenham notes that here the waters that were separate at creation come back to-gether (*Genesis 1–15*, 181). At creation the chaos waters are separated and order results. Here the waters come back together and chaos and death result.

13. Batto (*Slaying*, 86, 214) claims that the flood is not directly caused by God but by a rupture in the firmament and that Genesis 6:17 does not contradict this as it "has

Psalm 89 seems to pick up on this theme but with a delicacy that is extraordinary. The psalmist has clearly decided that God has broken promises made to the Davidic dynasty. The structure of the psalm produces a powerful lament. The reader hears the invective with which the psalm is prayed in its original context. The final stinging words lay the situation clearly at the feet of the Almighty as the psalmist attempts to cajole God into action.

However, the greater sting in this psalm is not this sting in the tail. Within the body of the psalm lies buried a promise that casts a shadow of ambiguity over the whole piece. Immediately prior to promising not to violate the covenant, God says (Ps 89:30–33):

> If his children forsake my law and do not walk according to my ordinances, if they violate my statutes and do not keep my commandments, then I will punish their transgression with the rod and their iniquity with scourges; but I will not remove from him my steadfast love, or be false to my faithfulness.

When the king protests in the lament, he never protests his innocence. Elsewhere psalmists protest innocence precisely to remind God that there are covenant obligations to save those who have kept their side of the deal (e.g., Ps 44:17–22). The coincidence of no protestation of innocence, the covenant promise to punish the unfaithful nation and king, and the situation of the king as recently abased suggest that maybe the king is not as innocent as he might wish the LORD God to assume he is.

The reader cannot help but wonder. Has God really abandoned the king and gone back on covenant promises? Or has God judged the sinfulness of the king with the full intention of remaining faithful to the covenant people in some future rescue from their present suffering? Is the king innocent of guilt and treated unfairly? Has the king the perfect right to blame God for divine failure? Or is the king blind to his own faults and screaming at the heavens in self-satisfied moral denial? Or is the king trying to twist the arm of God, fully aware of his failings but unwilling to admit them publicly?

The power of this psalm lies in its fascinating ambiguity. How much of this questioning (if any) the psalmist ever intended is difficult to tell. However, the inquisitive reader cannot help asking how verses 19–34 tie

---

reference not to the proximate cause of the flood but to God as the ultimate cause of all being." This is simply incorrect. The story clearly has God deciding to blot out humanity on account of its sinfulness (Gen 6:6–7, 17). The theology may be unpalatable to some but that is the theology of this text. Batto's Tillichian reading has no basis in the text.

up with verses 38–51. The psalmist seems to speak as the king throughout the psalm. Yet if we are to read the promise of divine punishment as part of covenant love and as unheard and unanswered by the king in his lament, then the psalmist seems to speak in another voice also. The psalmist as psalmist leaves the promise of discipline to echo across the invective of the lament to be heard by the inquisitive reader. Then the words "I will not violate my covenant" (Ps 89:34a) carry a double irony. The psalmist as king suggests in powerful lament that God has violated the covenant. The psalmist as psalmist suggests precisely that in disciplining the king through his present suffering God has kept his covenant promise.

Psalm 89 opens up questions that the reader may find difficult to answer. However, it does not shy away from suffering and presents an example of someone crying out to God bitterly and angrily from their pain. The psalmist does not spare the reader the pain but provides a language in which to explore frustrated disappointment. The language of the conquest of chaos is used not only to describe the action of God but also the action that God has promised to share with the king and by extension covenant people. The lack of this language in the lament is in itself telling—there is no conquest of chaos in the suffering, simply chaos and broken promises, or so it seems.

Reading the psalm with an attentive eye on the promise to chastise opens up space for the contemporary (if not the original) worshipper to explore the messy space of divine discipline and our reactions to it. We cannot be sure of the innocence or guilt of the king—though the lack of protestation may imply guilt. Whatever the truth, the cries of the sufferer are heard alongside a double-edged promise of God. Whether the present reality is evidence of the providence of God in chastising the errant or a demonstration of the mystery of God seeming to be absent and failing to maintain divine pledges, the promise of an eternal covenant gives hope for the future. But this hope for the future is not allowed to mask the suffering of the present where the psalmist gives the anguished king the last word. This combination of tensions provides space for readers to bring their own tangled webs of faith in suffering to their meditations on the psalm and their own spiritual lives. We are helped in the lack of resolution in the psalm to resist the temptation to all too easy (and possibly facile) resolutions in our own suffering. The final cry of accusation gives us space to live with our suffering until such time as genuine resolution might appear. However, this does not leave us in hopeless despair. The covenant-keeping faithfulness of

God may have been questioned but it has not been overturned. We are left with its echoes punctuating our meditations.

PSALM 77: LOOKING BACK IN HOPE

The psalmist cries out in anguish. He cries out day and night, continually bringing his complaint to God (Ps 77:2). His style of prayer involves meditating and moaning (Ps 77:3). He is determined to bring his complaint before God and meditate, and he is determined to bring before God how he feels about it and is not afraid of admitting that he cannot cope—"my spirit faints" (Ps 77:3). The psalmist models praying despair. In this he turns inwards, too troubled to speak (Ps 77:4). As prayer turns silent he turns over again and again in his mind and heart the question of whether God really is faithful or whether God has abandoned him (Ps 77:6–10). He refuses to accept easy answers (Ps 77:2d). With all this going round and round in his spirit, the psalmist cannot sleep (Ps 77:4).

The situation the psalmist faces is not described. The questions in verses 8–10 use terms like "steadfast love," which are used elsewhere of the relationship God has with the covenant people (e.g., Ps 89).[14] This might suggest that the situation concerning our psalmist is a crisis affecting the whole people of God.[15] However, this is slim evidence on which to suggest that the psalmist is petitioning God in time of national crisis as God can surely also be faithful and favorable to an individual—to which truth the story of Noah bears eloquent witness. It would be safer not to build an argument out of silence. There is no description of the situation facing the psalmist. There is also no indication that others are involved in a similar process of doubt and questioning. They appear to be alone in their despair.[16]

Interestingly the psalmist discovers the answer for which he is looking in the heart of his despairing thoughts. He is meditating on the "days of old" and the "years of long ago" (Ps 77:5). Presumably as he does this he is thinking through the mighty and miraculous actions of God to save the covenant people. He must be thinking on this or very similar lines to be wondering why God is no longer faithful—which is the essence of all his questions in

---

14. Hossfeld and Zenger, *Psalms 2*, 277–78.

15. Ibid., 274–75; Kraus, *Psalms 60–150*, 114.

16. Similarly, Goldingay (*Psalms 2*, 461) questions the consensus that the psalmist laments on behalf of the nation and suggests that this is in fact an individual lament.

verses 7–10.[17] The meditation the psalmist undertakes in misery becomes the key that unlocks his questioning and opens him up to hope once again.

Having asked the questions of God's faithfulness, the psalmist muses on the mighty acts of God and in doing so finds renewed hope. The psalmist thinks through the events of the exodus from Egypt and recounts them in full mythological color (Ps 77:16–20):

> When the waters saw you, O God, when the waters saw you, they were afraid; the very deep trembled. The clouds poured out waters; the skies thundered; your arrows flashed on every side. The crash of your thunder was in the whirlwind; your lightnings lit up the world; the earth trembled and shook. Your way was through the sea, your path, through the mighty waters; yet your footprints were unseen. You led your people by hand of Moses and Aaron.

The reference to Moses and Aaron ensures a reference to the exodus, not least when mentioning them in the same breath as making a path through waters. This text must at some level refer to the events of the Red (or Reed) Sea.[18] Nonetheless, the language used here goes beyond the accounts of the event in Exodus 14–15. The motifs used are unmistakably those of the myth of the divine warrior conquering the chaos waters. The waters were afraid at the sight of the divine warrior (Ps 77:16). The divine warrior opened fire on the sea from the cloud chariot, casting thunders, lightning, and whirlwind at the enemy (Ps 77:17–18). The happy ending for the covenant people being led through the Red Sea assumes that the divine warrior wins a victory over the sea.[19] The psalmist uses as much of the myth as necessary to picture the exodus events as a victory of God over the powers of chaos.

The psalm ends poignantly. The psalmist simply breaks off in the middle of reciting the wonderful saving acts of God. There is no evidence of a resolution. The psalmist does not move from petition to thanksgiving. We do not know whether he gave up his introspective wrangling with God at this point or whether he continued to wrestle with God in prayer until the

---

17. Similarly Hossfeld and Zenger, *Psalms 2*, 277; Goldingay, *Psalms 2*, 464.

18. Hossfeld and Zenger, *Psalms 2*, 279. On the question of the name, location, and historical reality of the sea (Red Sea, Reed Sea, or even Sea of Death), see Batto, "The Reed Sea: Requiescat in Pace"; Batto, "Red Sea or Reed Sea?"; and the response in Kitchen, *Reliability*, 261–63. Periodically, there are attempts at explaining this event in terms of natural causes. For a recent one, see Colin Humphries *Miracles in Exodus*. For a discussion of various attempts to reconstruct what happened at the exodus, see Kitchen, *Reliability*, 241–74.

19. Hossfeld and Zenger, *Psalms 2*, 279; Goldingay, *Psalms 2*, 468–71.

situation was resolved.[20] We do not even know whether the contemplation of the mighty acts of God soothed the tensions they experienced. We leave the psalm at the point at which the psalmist is beginning to recall these acts.

Again we find we have a psalm that gives us tension and space within it to explore our own reactions. The psalmist does not hold back from describing the despair he feels. He gives us a very clear picture of his reactions to his situation and how he suffers. He offers us a testimony of a movement he makes from introspection to meditation on the goodness of God. He leave us no clue as to how far he moves towards praise, although he clearly moves from despair to contemplating reasons for hope. The movement has a wonderful authenticity about it as it is not forced. The reason that the psalmist makes this movement is because his misery took him to the place where this path begins. Out of the disappointment, he wondered why God would not act as in ages past. This very contemplation transmuted itself into meditation on how God had acted in ages past, which the psalmist commits to thinking through.

I wonder what we learn from this psalm. Goldingay writes as others have spoken:[21]

> Refuse to be comforted; do not give in to acceptance too soon. . . .
> Think about God, about the days when you enjoyed God's blessing,
> about the praise you used to be able to offer. Face tough questions,
> and face the hurt. Remind yourself and remind God of the great
> things that God did in delivering us as his people at the beginning.
> Only if you do that can you look to God to give ear to you.

Much as there seems to be wisdom in such an interpretation, I wonder if this is more prescriptive than the psalm itself. Nobody told the psalmist to praise or to recount the mighty acts of God. Much as I think that such activity is to be highly recommended, I cannot help thinking that prescribing this activity to those in despair can sometimes be counterproductive. The testimony of the psalmist is one of touching the hem of grace. Out of nowhere, the very expression of their misery becomes the impetus for looking towards a more hopeful future and so they take the first tentative steps.

20. Goldingay (*Psalms 2*, 472–73) moves a little beyond the text here in suggesting that the psalm encourages worshippers to refuse to be comforted. The psalmist leaves us with more ambiguity than Goldingay admits.

21. Goldingay, *Psalms 2*, 473. He sums up an interpretation I have heard at countless study groups and in not a few sermons much as I remain unconvinced that this psalm is quite so prescriptive.

Perhaps the real lessons of this psalm (if any) are different. The psalmist sets an example in being honest about how he experiences his suffering. He opens himself up fully to God. He has the courage to take his first faltering steps on a more hopeful path when it presents itself. I would like to suggest that the "nowhere" from which the first rays of hope sprang was the providence of God—but that would be an argument out of silence.

PSALM 144

Not all those who need God's help cry out from a place of anguish. Psalm 144 offers the prayer of a psalmist who is unusually cheerful for someone who needs deliverance from his enemies. The psalmist opens by blessing God for training him in the art of war and enabling him to defeat his enemies (Ps 144:1–2). However, this is no ruse that will lead to a sting later on as with the hymn of praise that opens Psalm 89. The psalmist follows with an expression of awe and wonder that the immortal God condescends to take the time to even consider transient creatures like human beings (Ps 144:3–4).

At this point the psalmist moves from blessing and praise to petition (Ps 144:5–8):

> Bow your heavens, O LORD, and come down; touch the mountains so that they smoke. Make the lightning flash and scatter them; send out your arrows and rout them. Stretch out your hand from on high; set me free and rescue me from the mighty waters, from the hand of aliens, whose mouths speak lies, and whose right hands are false.

This is no lament.[22] The psalmist does not complain about what his enemies have done or about what he fears his enemies might do. Although the psalmist appears to be in trouble, he does not moan that God has failed to keep any promises nor does he ask God how long the situation will remain difficult for him. They simply petition God.

The language of the petition is familiar. Indeed it recalls Psalm 18, another in which God the divine warrior was summoned to the aid of the

---

22. Despite previous attempts to identify this psalm as of one genre or another (e.g., Kraus [*Psalms 60–150*, 541] who classifies it as a song of prayer and thanksgiving), recent commentators tend to identify it as mixed form—so Hossfeld and Zenger, *Psalms 3*, 583; Schaefer, *Psalms*, 336.

psalmist.[23] God must bend the heavens again and come down (Ps 144:5a recalling Ps 18:9). Touching the mountains so they smoke probably refers to Ps 18:8–9 (Ps 144:5b). God must fight the enemy with lightning (Ps 144:6 recalling Ps 18:14). Picturing himself as caught in the torrent of the chaos waters, the psalmist asks for the divine warrior to rescue him (Ps 144:7 recalling Ps 18:16). By putting them in parallel, the psalmist identifies the chaos waters with his enemies who seek to do him harm (Ps 144:7c–8). The psalmist uses the familiar language of the divine warrior defeating chaos to ask God to perform another mighty act in rescuing him from his enemies.

There follows a promise to praise God as the one who rescues the Davidic king (Ps 144:9–10). Then the psalmist makes a final petition for rescue from his enemies but again without complaint (Ps 144:11). Without a hint of complaint the psalmist pronounces a formal blessing on the covenant people that their children might be healthy, that the land might be prosperous, and that the land might be safe from its enemies (Ps 144:12–14). The psalm ends with a final blessing, which may contain a hint of a request that the blessings of verses 12–14 materialize but which also ends the psalm on a note of confident faith that God will achieve this for the covenant people because that is what the LORD God is like (Ps 144:15).

Psalm 144 takes at least a couple of old songs, mixes them up a bit, and strikes up a new tune. The references to Psalm 18 are hardly accidental as there are too many to pass off as coincidence.[24] However, the psalmist does something quite new with the old material. Whoever first sang Psalm 18 was giving thanks to God for *already* having come in victory to defeat the chaos waters (i.e., the psalmist's enemies) and having put them in a good place. Whoever made the cover we know as Psalm 144 gave thanks in advance of the rescue, blessing God for the covenant promises, and petitioning God to fulfill them—but most of all blessing God, as blessings frame the whole psalm. Psalm 144 turns the thanksgivings of Psalm 18 for *past* acts into a statement of faith in the goodness of God's nature and a consequent petition for *future* deliverance. The cover version does something novel with the original.

Psalm 144 also takes and uses rather differently the divine warrior motif. This had been used in earlier psalms to impressive rhetorical effect in laments and sometimes with great invective. The song of divine deliverance (originally such a happy one) has become quite a sad song in the likes

23. Hossfeld and Zenger, *Psalms 2*, 585–86.

24. Hossfeld and Zenger, *Psalms 3*, 584–88; Kraus, *Psalms 60–150*, 541.

of Psalms 74 and 89. This is understandable. The vision of the Zion psalms (like Psalm 46) that spoke of God's control out of chaos ensuring that Jerusalem would never fall was proven defective (or at the very least not the whole story) by the events of the Babylonian invasion of Judah in the sixth century BC. So the song becomes one of angry protest. In Psalm 144 the psalmist changes the tune once again. The song becomes one of hope again but one that remains open to the future. There is no sense of an inviolably perfect future whatever peril assails us (as in Psalm 46).[25] Instead there is the tentative confidence of one who trusts God but recognizes the difficulties of the present and is unafraid to address God with the need for change. There is recognition of suffering (as in Psalms 74 and 89) but the reaction to this is not to blame God for failure but to bless God for what lies at the heart of the divine personality.

There are many more psalms presenting many more laments and using the divine warrior motif to speak of the psalmists' relationships with God. The ones we have studied have focused specifically on how people have handled their suffering in the presence of God. These psalms have all witnessed to the honesty of the worshippers in pouring out their hearts and souls before God. Nothing of what is felt and known is hidden. The psalmists offer ways of praying that model authentic and honest spirituality. Ritual lament, crying out before God in community and as individuals, seems to have been natural to the psalmists. However, the psalms we have examined do not simply model the expression of anger, much as they are not afraid of expressing anger. They offer examples of the ambiguity of prayer from suffering. These psalms are not in this way didactic, instructing us that these are good models to follow when we are angry or sensing that God has let us down. The psalms model a freedom and authenticity of expression that is spiritually more freeing and ultimately more honest. But they are truthful and faithful beyond our self-expression. They raise the question of who really is in the right when we feel let down by God and they do not answer this—leaving open the possibility that we ourselves might be in the wrong. Nor do they require us to be angry in response to our suffering. They allow for the possibility that we might want to suffer from a place of praise and confidence in the faithfulness of God.

25. For the record, I actually like Psalm 46!

4

WRESTLING WITH
AN ABSENT ALMIGHTY

ANY WHO VENTURE INTO the book of Job and carefully watch the ways of its monsters may notice that our dragons have a twist in their tale. God does not always appear to win. Feisty little creatures that they are, they can wreak so much havoc that it can appear that evil has conquered good. Our dragons can terrify and destroy. Indeed chaos and evil can so overwhelm someone that they can wish they were dead—that Leviathan would stop toying with them, and would simply come and finish them off. The humble believer can become so embittered in her suffering that she can wonder whether God is confused. People can ask whether maybe, in some kind of celestial short-sightedness, the Almighty has muddled the monster with them and declared war on the good rather than destroying evil. Sometimes God can come across as very slow to manifest his great love in reality, and we are left asking the question of how long we will suffer, or whether in fact we will ever see an end to our pain. But things are not always what they seem. The spirituality of the book of Job explores all these experiences and more. We will work our way through Job's own struggles with God in prayer and fellowship. However, before going in any deeper, it is necessary to get a handle on the basic storyline or we will run the risk of losing the plot.

SETTING THE SORRY SCENE

God has made a deal with the satan.[1] The latter wandered into the divine council one day and just mentioned how Job only really worshipped God for what he could get out of God. God disagreed and allowed the satan to take away the health, wealth, and children with which Job had been blessed in order to test whether he truly worshipped God (Job 1:1—2:8). Sitting in ashes and attempting to come to terms with his loss of both prosperity and posterity, his wife urging him on to curse God and die, Job is unaware of why any of this has happened to him (Job 2:8–10). Three old friends come and sit with him in total silence for seven days, sharing in his shock (Job 2:11–13).[2] After this, Job can contain himself no longer. At this point the book moves from being a tale in prose to arguments in poetry.

Job complains about his situation and his friends try offering explanations and advice. They urge him to honor and respect God. Job answers them from and with his own experience asks them how this fits with their explanations. He challenges them by pointing out that standard teachings about suffering do not fit in his case. He demands that they stretch their theological imaginations to try and work out how God could possibly be righteous and allow *his* suffering—given that God is supposed to reward, not destroy, the righteous. The conversation becomes quite tense and rather terse. Tempers fray and in a magnificent last speech, Job challenges *God* to explain what he has done to deserve this suffering (Job 31:1–40). God responds from the whirlwind and converses with Job. The way the book is laid out suggests that this final conversation between God and Job somehow resolves at least some of the issues at some level. Exactly how remains the subject of dispute amongst many readers of Job.[3]

---

1. The Hebrew *haśśāṭān* ought probably to be translated "the satan" or "the accuser." It is not a personal name but a title that depicts this figure as the prosecuting attorney on the divine council. His job is to check that people are truly righteous. See further Clines, *Job 1-20*, 18–23; Day, *Adversary*.

2. Job's comforters are possibly as misrepresented as the Pharisees. They may later argue theological cases that seem untenable as explications of Job's suffering but surely their initial reaction is spot on. Would that all who have uttered the words "Job's comforters" showed such pastoral sensitivity.

3. What I write below is unlikely to resolve the issues surrounding the interpretation of the divine speeches. Of this I am fully aware. However, I hope it offers a useful perspective for consideration by those who meditate on the mysteries of this remarkable and in many ways unsettling book.

Job is something of a courtroom drama.[4] Job wants to have his day in court with God. He still sort of believes that God will ultimately bless the righteous and punish the evil but trying to get God to do this is not that simple. Job demands to have it out with God in court but despairs that no one can summon God to court and even if they tried, God simply would not listen (Job 9:2–35). Nevertheless, Job prepares his case because he is sure that he will win. He even shouts at God to come to court and face the challenge (Job 13:13–28). Later, crying out from despair Job claims in desperation that he knows that someone in the divine council will defend his case and he pleads that God will hear before he dies (Job 16:18–22). Insistent that he has been mistreated, Job cries that a permanent record of the injustice he has suffered be made and he reaffirms his belief that someone on the divine council will one day finally speak up for him and call God to account for the injustice he has suffered (Job 19:23–7). His suffering continues and his friends fail to see his innocence or recognize his point. Job continues to insist on his day in court so that hearing his case, God might acquit him (Job 23:1–7). Before finally falling silent, Job cries out one last time that God would at least tell him what he has done wrong and once more he demands the opportunity to come before God in the divine council and protest his innocence (31:35–37). The greater part of the drama of Job is the speeches between Job and his friends and between Job and God. Job's insistence of his innocence drives the drama and finally provokes an appearance from the Almighty. God speaks. The case is decided. God appears to win.

Then the book moves back from poetic speeches to the tale in prose. The argument is over. The court case is won and now reparation must be made. But there is a twist in the tale. Curiously God commends Job for speaking rightly (Job 42:7). God underlines this by stating how the friends have not spoken rightly by comparison. God asks Job to pray for his friends so that they are not punished as their foolishness deserves. Then God showers rewards for his righteousness on Job. God does not seem to approve of judging people's experiences according to standard doctrines if those doctrines do not fit. As the book stands, it invites the reader to take a closer look at what God really values in the spirituality of the suffering.

4. Habel, *Job*, 54–56.

THE CURIOUS CASE OF A LEVIATHAN SANDWICH

Another curious fact about Job is that the speeches start and end with Leviathan. When Job lets rip for the first time, one of the ways in which he expresses his anguish is to curse the day he was born and in doing so refers to Leviathan (Job 3:8). When God makes his second and final speech in response to Job, he ends up talking about Leviathan (Job 41:1–34). These speeches start and end the speech section of Job. So Leviathan forms an inclusion around, or frames, the whole of the speech section in Job. At the very least, this ought to alert the reader to the possibility that the myths about Leviathan might be a lens the author is asking us to look through in reading the speeches. Interestingly the use of the divine warrior motif occurs more in Job than in other books, which again suggests to the reader that it might not be merely a literary ornament but have something to do with the plot or meaning of the book. Also rather interesting is the fact that the only two characters to use the myth in the book are Job and God.[5] The exclusive use of the myth by Job and God, its comparative commonness in the book as compared with other biblical books, and its being used to frame the speech section in Job suggest that the author of Job asks the readers to pay some attention to the use of the myth in this book in attempting to understand whatever it is trying to say about suffering.

Shouting at a Distant Deity

At the opening of the speech section, Job cries out in despair (Job 3:3–11):

> Let the day perish in which I was born, and the night that said, "A man-child is conceived." Let that day be darkness! May God above not seek it, or light shine on it. Let gloom and deep darkness claim it. Let clouds settle upon it; let the blackness of the day terrify it. That night—let thick darkness seize it! Let it not rejoice among the days of the year; let it not come into the number of the months. Yes, let that night be barren; let no joyful cry be heard in it. Let those curse it who curse the day, those who are skilled to rouse up Leviathan. Let the stars of its dawn be dark; let it hope for light, but have none; may it not see the eyelids of the morning—because it did not shut the doors of my mother's womb, and hide trouble from my eyes. Why did I not die at birth, come forth from the womb and expire?

5. I do not accept the re-allocation of Job 26:5–14 to Bildad. See below.

Job rues the day he was born. He asks that the day be darkness and light perish. He envisages the stars losing their light and the day losing its place in the fixed order of days and months. Some have seen in this a reversal of creation motif. The order of creation involved stars giving light, calendrical order, and the distinguishing between night and day.[6] Creation saw God make the chaos monsters in Genesis 1:1—2:3 and some versions of the myth saw them conquered. Here Job asks for those who can rouse the chaos monster Leviathan to come and create chaos out of order. He refers to some kind of magician who would be able to summon the forces of chaos and evil to wreak their work of havoc in destroying the day he was born.[7]

Job does not begin with the kind of lament we have seen in a number of the psalms. He does not remind God of the time at creation when God defeated the chaos dragon. Job does not ask for Leviathan to be killed afresh. The bitterness of the darker psalms is present but without the hope that God might be cajoled into action to conquer chaos again. Instead the opening action suggests that enchanters should wipe his day of birth out of history using language that has undertones of the undoing of creation.

This twist on tradition may be understandable in the light of the moral aesthetic that lies at the heart of wisdom. Lady Wisdom has been with God throughout creation and together they have designed an order that flourishes when people live righteous lives (Prov 1–9).[8] Job has lived righteously

---

6. Fishbane, "Jeremiah IV 23–26 and Job III 3–13." See also Habel, *Job*, 106–7; Hartley, *Job*, 88. Clines (*Job 1–20*, 81), however, is dismissive of the idea but admits the central tenet that Job wishes for his universe (even if not the whole universe) to cease to exist and uses some cosmic language to do this. Moreover, his assertion that rousing Leviathan is not a reversal of the creation of sea monsters seems to miss the *theological* reversal that takes place here: instead of God creating and so having control over the chaos monsters as in Genesis 1, Job longs for the monsters to come and take things back to chaos. This is a reversal motif.

7. For the background on enchanters summoning chaos monsters in the ancient Near East, see Fishbane "Recovered Use." Fyall (*Now my Eyes*, 59) over-interprets Job 3:8 when he suggests that Job intends to "uncreate" (so also, Fishbane, "Recovered Use," 153, whose suggestion that Job "binds spell to spell in his articulation of an absolute death wish for himself and the entire creation" oversteps the boundaries of what the text says). Job intends no such thing. Job only wishes the day of his birth were eradicated from time and creation in order that he might not be suffering. Job uses undoing of creation language to refer only to the undoing of this day, although the allusive use of this language lends dark undertones to the lament. Contrary to the NRSV, I read "day" instead of "Sea" in this text as the MT text reads "day." For an argument for retaining the MT, see Day, *God's Conflict*, 46–47.

8. Fox, "Epistemology."

(Job 1:1). However, the rewards of the righteous are no longer his. The suffering he has undergone stretches his understanding of the moral aesthetic beyond the boundary. He cannot see that his righteousness has been rewarded but rather the calamities of the wicked and worse have been visited upon him. Job wants to die.

In order to express this sentiment, Job takes the language of the lament tradition of the psalms and subverts it. He uses the language so often used to cajole God into re-creation to express his desire to have creation undone in his own life. Rather than ask God to recreate, he asks that magicians or enchanters (those who practice dark arts that God would not countenance) do their ungodly (indeed opposite of godly) work of turning creation back to chaos. Job throws down the gauntlet. He expresses his feelings that God cannot be trusted to create out of chaos and so it is better to turn to enchanters to create chaos and death.

Job does not show any of his proverbial patience. He complains bitterly about his treatment at God's hand. Reflecting on his experience, he concludes that there is no hope. God clearly does not reward the righteous. There is no justice in the world—at least for him. He has lost almost everything. Therefore, it is better to die. He expresses this eloquently in the poetry of the biblical tradition: if God has handed him over to chaos and evil, then let Leviathan swallow him up that he might die and his suffering end.

Railing into the Divine Silence

Job uses the myth again to rail against the perceived injustice of God. Job prays: "am I the Sea or the Dragon that you set a guard over me?" (Job 7:12).[9] Here Job compares himself to the sea (the Hebrew word for sea, *yam*, recalls the Canaanite sea god Yammu of Ugaritic lore) and the dragon. The motif of the imprisonment of the dragon is found in other ancient Near Eastern texts. Yammu was at one time the captive of Ba'lu (*KTU* 1.2 iv 29–30). Marduk imprisons Tiamat and her monstrous hordes (*Enuma Elish* IV 110–14). Ancient Near Eastern gods imprison the dragon after

9. Dahood ("Muzzle") proposed the translation "muzzle" instead of "guard." Barr ("Ugaritic and Hebrew," 17–39) demonstrated that this translation rests on insecure foundations. The idea that Job presents God as trying to prevent him from speaking and taking his complaint to the divine council would make sense here (against Clines, *Job 1–20*, 165) but the philological grounds for making this case are weak. Moreover the Greek (LXX) and Latin (Vulgate) translations support the translation "guard" over "muzzle."

they defeat it in battle. The motif is also found in Hebrew tradition (*Pr. Man.* 3).[10]

Placing himself in the shoes of the imprisoned dragon, Job makes an extraordinary theological statement. He states as a righteous and (erstwhile) god-fearing man that God has made him his enemy. God hates and attacks him as much as God does the primeval chaos monsters that God slaughtered or imprisoned at creation. This is quite some accusation! Not only does he suggest that God has not rewarded his righteousness, he states that God has treated him as if he were the personification or incarnation of chaos itself.

For those who know the tradition, this subverts its central theme even further than his calling upon magicians to rouse Leviathan to recreate chaos. When God the divine warrior comes in theophany to defeat evil, God rescues the righteous person and delivers him or her from the clutches of the monster or the torrents of the chaos waters. Here instead Job identifies the righteous man, namely himself, as the enemy of God. God treats the righteous as the powers of evil and so turns divine justice on its head. Job asks God a question that in turn questions the very nature of God as righteous.

In one sense Job has hit a spiritual low. He simply does not have the faith that enables him to see God as just or active. His experience suggests that God has withheld divine justice, and allowed both evil to triumph and Job to suffer. In another sense, Job shows remarkable spiritual maturity. His faith has always been in a just God. He knows decisions are taken in the divine council to ensure justice on earth. His very protest against God demonstrates the depth and solidity of his belief in justice at this point. He can only question the justice of God because of the strength of his expectation that God will be just. And so he asks the pointed question but the only answer he receives is that of divine silence.

Questioning God's Motives

Job lets God know exactly how he feels. He suffers so badly he wants to die. He has lost hope that God can or will rescue him. He questions divine justice. Now Job wonders whether the language of God saving people masks an altogether more disturbing reality (Job 9:2–14):

10. Angel, *Chaos*, 82.

> Indeed I know that this is so; but how can a mortal be just before God? If one wished to contend with him, one could not answer him once in a thousand. He is wise in heart, and mighty in strength—who has resisted him, and succeeded?—he who removes mountains, and they do not know it, when he overturns them in his anger; who shakes the earth out of its place, and its pillars tremble; who commands the sun, and it does not rise; who seals up the stars; who alone stretched out the heavens and trampled the waves of the Sea; who made the Bear and Orion, the Pleiades and the chambers of the south; who does great things beyond understanding, and marvelous things without number. Look, he passes by me, and I do not see him; he moves on, but I do not perceive him. He snatches away; who can stop him? Who will say to him, "What are you doing?" God will not turn back his anger; the helpers of Rahab bowed beneath him. How then can I answer him, choosing my words with him?

Job speaks of the power of God to move mountains, shake the earth to its very foundations, and change the ordering of the heavenly luminaries. God trampling the waves of the sea refers to God conquering chaos.[11] The picture of the helpers of Rahab cowering before God depicts either their imminent defeat by God or their imprisonment after God has beaten them in battle. This is all standard theophanic language. Job asks what hope he has against God in court. If God is as strong as the language of theophany suggests, then Job rightly notes that he has little chance of winning his case. God is simply too wise and too mighty and nobody wins against God (Job 9:4).[12]

The use of the language of the divine warrior here is surely ironic. Insofar as we can reconstruct the myth on which the biblical writers drew, it seems to have gone something like this. The righteous person or the righteous people are in some kind of trouble. God the divine warrior rides the heavenly cloud chariot from the heavenly court to the place on earth where the battle with chaos needs to be fought to rescue the righteous. As God comes to earth, various heavenly and earthly portents occur, which may include the moving of celestial bodies from their normal places in the heavens, the shaking of the foundations of the earth, and mountains trembling and smoking. God then defeats the waters or dragons of chaos if they have

---

11. Day, *God's conflict*, 42.

12. Similarly, Clines, *Job 1–20*, 232–33; Habel, *Job*, 190–92; Hartley, *Job*, 168–76. Gordis sees this as a sardonic use of the traditional language of the power of God (*Job*, 522), a viewpoint developed in the reading below.

not already fled in terror. At this point there is sometimes mention of God creating the structures of the world and the heavens.

Job plays on this theophanic pattern. He follows partway and then suddenly moves off in a strange new direction. The normal theophanic portents of a trembling earth are mentioned (Job 9:5–6). The disturbances in the heavens are described (Job 9:7). Then Job speaks of God's conquest of the sea (Job 9:8). The following description of the work of creation after the conquest of chaos completes the picture (Job 9:9–10). However, at this point the theophany moves in an unconventional direction. God continues in the march to battle with the powers of chaos, passing Job by (Job 9:11–12) before going to terrify the demonic band of helpers who accompany the chaos monster Rahab (Job 9:13).[13]

One cannot help asking why Job depicts God marching on to terrify the helpers of Rahab after conquering chaos in verse 8. What is the virtue of marching into battle when chaos has already been conquered? Why conquer chaos twice (assuming God terrifying the helpers of Rahab refers to some sort of victory over them or arrival to defeat them in battle)? Job plays around with the traditional script.

But Job does not simply play around with the story. He plays around with the theology and the language of the theophany. Job talks of God passing by (Job 9:11). "Passing by" is the language of 1 Kgs 19:11–13 where God promises to appear to Elijah. It is the language of Exod 33:32–33 where God appears to Moses in the theophany.[14] When God passes by, God reveals something of the divine power and glory to faithful people. The theophany often signals that God will rescue faithful servants from troubles

13. Commentators note some unevenness in the flow of this hymn and suggest rearrangements of its verses or try to justify its current arrangement, e.g., Hartley (*Job*, 170) who tries to justify bringing the element of personal lament in verse 11 into a hymn of praise. Gordis (*Job*, 105) suggests that the unevenness reflects "the spirit of biblical and Oriental poetry, with its rapidly shifting emotions and attitudes." Clines (*Job 1–20*, 229–33) simply sees a shift from a hymn of praise in verses 5–11 to an acknowledgment of God's anger in verses 11–13. The use of divine warrior imagery in verse 13 suggests continuity with verse 5–10 where the same language is found. Hence the suggestion here that Job manipulates the form of the divine warrior hymn to make his point.

14. However, there are distinct differences between Job and these texts. Against Hartley (*Job*, 173), there is no straightforward parallel with 1 Kgs 19:11–13. There God does not appear in the classical portents of the theophany. Job (*Job* 9:5–13) assumes that God does appear in these classical portents—God just takes no notice of Job. Clines (*Job 1–20*, 232) suggests that Job not seeing God may be compared to Moses not seeing the face of God (Exod 33:32–33). This is implausible as Moses does see the back of God which entails seeing God whereas Job claims not to see God.

that assail them. However, God does not do this here. God passes Job by but Job does not see him. Seeing means seeing salvation (Job 19:26; 42:5b).[15] Job sees anything but his salvation at the hand of God. Job turns the language of theophany on its head. When God passes by, God is supposed to save. When God passes Job by, he fails to do anything of the sort.

Putting all this together, we begin to see the ironic invective of Job at this point. God comes in theophany with all the usual portents, defeats chaos and subsequently creation appears according to the normal pattern. At this point Job departs from the script. Instead of moving to praise God for the glorious work of defeating chaos and creating the world, he has God carry on with the march of the divine warrior. He uses the language of the theophany in talking of God passing by. He paints a picture of nobody being able to stop him in his march. Those watching God pass by want to ask why God is doing this—when chaos has been conquered already, why would the divine warrior continue in his march to battle? However, nobody dares ask the question. God drives on angrily towards the helpers of Rahab in order to terrify them (even though chaos has already been defeated, which begs the question of whether there is any point to further terrifying any chaos monsters).

Job undermines the theology of this language with bitter poignancy. God does come in theophany but is not interested in rescuing the righteous. God is only interested in destroying and terrifying chaos monsters. God comes across as angry, obsessed with theophany, and wholly unconcerned about rescuing the righteous.

This use of the language is surely ironic. The psalms most often use the language of the theophany of the divine warrior to depict God ordering creation with righteousness and justice or to cajole God to re-order creation along those lines, particularly for the covenant people. Job uses the very same language to say that God is too powerful and busy to bother to re-order anything for anyone as insignificant as the odd righteous man like himself. This is a deeply subversive and highly emotive use of the language. Even in the bitterest laments, the psalmists expect God to have the faithfulness to turn up and rescue them. Job moves the language onto another plane altogether. He freely acknowledges the power of God and suggests

---

15. Seeing does not mean literally seeing. This misunderstanding results in interpretive gymnastics where one tries to prove how Job can both see God pass by (and so know God has passed by) and not see God at the same time: so e.g., Clines (*Job 1–20*, 232) who tries to equate seeing God's back with not seeing God, an explanation that involves a certain measure of self-contradiction.

that precisely because God is so powerful, God does not care much about the responsibilities that come with divine power. Power corrupts. Divine power makes monsters out of gods. Within these few lines of poetry, Job suggests that God is too busy fighting mythical monsters to care about real human beings.

Mere Whispers of Divinity

Job's friends are none too impressed. The dialogue continues and Job moves his complaint forward to the point where he asks his friends to look beyond his own suffering to the many righteous people in this world who suffer and to whom God seems to pay no attention (Job 24:1–25). He throws this observation down as something of a gauntlet before his friends, asking them why God does not notice the suffering righteous and whether they can really look around at reality and claim that there is no force to his complaint.

Bildad responds with confident dogmatism. God reigns in heaven and commands the armies of angels. God is glorious beyond human imagining and therefore nobody can be pure in his sight (Job 25:2–6). Job responds with biting sarcasm (Job 26:2–14):[16]

> How you have helped one who has no power! How you have assisted the arm that has no strength! How you have counseled one who has no wisdom, and given much good advice! With whose help have you uttered words, and whose spirit has come forth from you? The shades below tremble, the waters and their inhabitants. Sheol is naked before God, and Abaddon has no covering. He stretches out Zaphon over the void, and hangs the earth

16. There is a critical issue concerning who speaks verses 5–14. The text ascribes them to Job. However, some authors find their character out of keeping. Against, e.g., Dhorme (*Job*, xlvii–l), Gordis (*Job*, 278–81), Habel (*Job*, 364–75) and Clines (*Job* 21-37, 634) I do not read these verses as belonging to Bildad. Hartley (*Job*, 368) argues for their belonging to Job on the basis that Job uses hymnic language in praise of God elsewhere in the book and does so here to keep his pecker up. This does not seem a very strong argument given the bitterness of Job's language in the nearby context. It is hard to imagine Job dropping his vitriol with God in order to sing a quick hymn of praise before resuming his tirade against God. However, I find it difficult to imagine Bildad saying the line in Job 26:14 which clearly belongs as the climax of Job 26:5-14. The Bildad who confidently asserts that God will act to save and that Job will see it (Job 8:20–22), who asserts that in the present the justice of God in punishing the wicked is everywhere in evidence (Job 18:2–21) is much more likely to end his speeches by calling Job a worm who cannot see God, as in the MT (Job 25:2–6), than by climbing down to the anticlimactic statement that we hardly hear a whisper of God's ways in reality (Job 26:14).

upon nothing. He binds up the waters in his thick clouds, and the cloud is not torn open by them. He covers the face of the full moon, and spreads over it his cloud. He has described a circle on the face of the waters, at the boundary between light and darkness. The pillars of heaven tremble, and are astounded at his rebuke. By his power he stilled the Sea; by his understanding he struck down Rahab. By his wind the heavens were made fair; his hand pierced the fleeing serpent. These are indeed but the outskirts of his ways; and how small a whisper do we hear of him! But the thunder of his power who can understand?

Again Job uses the language of theophany.[17] The trembling of the shades and the pillars of heaven traditionally accompanied the march of the divine warrior (Job 26:5, 11). The stilling of the Sea and the striking down of Rahab refer to the conquest of the forces of chaos by God (Job 26:11–12). Piercing the fleeing serpent recalls both Isa 27:1 and the Ugaritic myth where Leviathan the fleeing serpent is killed (Job 26:13; *KTU* 1.5 i 29–30).

Whatever Job does intend to say by this speech, he certainly does not intend to give Bildad the slightest impression that there is any truth in his out of touch and overly optimistic dogmatism. Bildad has pictured God in heaven surrounded by the heavenly armies whence he rules and orders the universe (Job 25:2–3). On this basis Bildad asserts that nobody has any right to question God—least of all Job (or at least he seems to imply this). Job tears into Bildad with a volley of sarcasm. First, Job tells Bildad how much (in reality, how little) his words have helped him or would help any of the suffering righteous Job named in his earlier speech (Job 26:2–3). Then Job asks Bildad where his wisdom comes from with an undertone (I suspect) of suggesting that it does not come from God. Job moves to describe God in theophanic glory, picking up Bildad's picture of God ruling from heaven surrounded by the armies of angels (Job 26:5–13). Job admits that these are the ways of God (Job 26:14a). In this, Job takes Bildad seriously at the level of religious language and doctrine. He affirms the creed that Bildad repeats: "these are indeed the outskirts of his ways" (Job 26:14a).

However, Job adds two small caveats from his own lived experience of faith. Whilst he admits that God does appear in glorious theophany and that God conquers chaos and creates a wonderful world, Job notes that God does not seem to do that glorious work much in his neighborhood: "and how small a whisper do we hear of him!" (Job 26:14b). The rebuke is

---

17. Gordis, *Job*, 280–81.

genuinely ironic. Job affirms that this is the work of God but currently he only recognizes this work by its absence. The statements Bildad makes are fruitless because they do not in any way integrate talk of God and the reality of suffering, and so Bildad fails to answer Job's questions—let alone those of anyone else who has suffered.

Job follows this by a statement of longing despair or perhaps nascent disengagement with the old creed: "but the thunder of his power who can understand?" (Job 26:14c). The old creed (as witnessed in the psalms) has God thunder from the heavens and rescue the righteous. The sound of thunder from heaven signals salvation on earth. Job affirms that God thunders but (as he states in his previous speech [Job 9:5–14]) God currently seems to have a tendency to thunder past the troubled righteous. Divine thunder has become an empty noise. Job can state the theoretical truth of the theophany but he clings onto any faith he has that God will ever do anything by a thread. God no longer seems to act the way he should and Job no longer understands.

This speech offers a magnificent example of human disengagement with God on account of weariness and despair in the face of God's absence. Job has struggled in prayer and has begged God for justice. Job has cried out from the very depths of his soul for God to act like God—to establish justice and reward the righteous. Job begs God for a day in court where he can hear of his guilt or establish his innocence. Job lays himself bare before the Almighty and asks for nothing more than recognition. Surely human beings are worth that basic respect in the eyes of a God who made them the pinnacle of creation? However, the divine silence has worn Job down. He is coming to the end of his capacity to cry out.

The conversation continues a little longer. Job states his longing for the old days when God truly acted like God and his righteousness was respected and rewarded (Job 29:1–25). Job moves to restate his complaint and to protest his innocence again (30:1—31:40). Before he falls silent once more, Job cries out for his day in court demanding again that God listen to his case in the divine council and prove that he deserves this suffering (Job 31:35–37).

Answering Back

And God replies from the whirlwind (Job 38:1). Answering Job from the midst of the storm suggests that the longed for theophany has come. God will put his case and Job will have his day in court. At the outset God challenges Job to gird up his loins like a hero or warrior.[18] Whether or not God characterizes the question-and-answer session that follows as some kind of fight, God begins the conversation with warrior language. The theophanic language used is probably no coincidence given what follows.

God Versus Job: Round One

In the first divine speech (Job 38:1—39:30) God asks Job who created and sustains creation—the answer being that it was God and not Job, with the firm implication that God does do this work. Towards the beginning of this speech, God asks Job (Job 38:8–11):

> Or who shut in the sea with doors when it burst out from the womb?—when I made the clouds its garment, and thick darkness its swaddling band, and prescribed bounds for it, and set bars and doors, and said, "Thus far shall you come, and no farther, and here shall your proud waves be stopped"?

The image of making boundaries for the sea recalls the conquest of chaos. On defeating the unruly waters, God set limits to them.[19] The same may be observed in the creation story where the waters are set above the skies and below the earth (Gen 1:6–8) and in the *Enuma Elish* where Marduk sets the waters of Tiamat in place (*Enuma Elish* IV 139–40, V 54–59). God affirms his conquest of chaos and his creation of the world. God asks Job where he was when God was conquering chaos, containing it and prevents it from over-spilling its bounds to the detriment of the created order. God challenges the right of Job to ask whether God really does conquer chaos, and make and sustain creation.

The rest of the first divine speech follows from exactly this point. Just as God conquered chaos, so God created and sustains creation. God consistently challenges Job, asking him whether he has made or sustained creation. The implication is that Job has done neither of these things. God asks Job if he knows the workings of the universe and again the implication is that whilst Job does not, God does know them.

---

18. The Hebrew *gibbor* can simply mean "man," but here the meaning "hero" or "warrior" most probably applies, so Habel, *Job*, 520–21.

19. Day, *God's Conflict*, 42–43; Clines, *Job 38–42*, 1101.

This speech has been interpreted in various ways. Bob Fyall suggests that God tries to imprint on the mind of Job the awesomeness of creation and the reality of life. Just as creation is magnificent, so it is tragic. Various images reveal that tragedy and suffering are inextricably part of creation. Goats give birth only to become bereft of their offspring (Job 39:1–4). The war horse engages in battle (Job 39:19–25). The eagle kills its prey (Job 39:26–30). Fyall suggests that Job teaches that suffering is part and parcel of life, and that creation is therefore somehow tragic.[20] However, such an interpretation assumes that the author of Job shared the sentimentalism towards nature that many moderns have. This would be a mistake. The goats successfully raising their young is a picture of success. The magnificence of the warhorse in battle is unlikely to have been an offensive or tragic image in a society that celebrated military victory as a gift from God. The sight of birds of prey hunting still draws admiration from many today and can more easily be read here as celebrating the impressiveness of these creatures. The celebration may not suit the sentimentalism of contemporary tastes but God celebrates creation in this text.

Gregory Mobley suggests that the first divine speech sets up what appears more fully in the second, which is that God has made a covenant with chaos. He suggests that chaos is part of the divine plan. It allows for creativity, which in turn opens up the possibility of love.[21] Although "love conquers all" can and does inspire some people to work through suffering, this does not appear to be what God says here in Job. God affirms that chaos has been conquered and been put under control (Job 38:8–11). However, this differs widely from making a covenant with chaos in which chaos has any degree of freedom.

Alternatively, God's reply in the first divine speech might suggest that God shows Job no respect. David Clines suggests that the speech certainly makes for masterful rhetoric and impresses upon the reader the awesome nature of the divine design but it completely ignores the concerns Job has raised. God does not answer any of his questions and in doing so appears high-handed and uninterested in righteous humanity.[22] Maybe God really is the God of Bildad (Job 25:2–6). The point has power and can easily be read from the text. However, I wish to suggest an alternative reading.

---

20. Fyall, *Now My Eyes*, 73–81.

21. Mobley, *Return*, 121–26.

22. Clines, *Job 38–42*, 1134–36.

In answering Job, God seems to go back to Job's original complaint. Job suffers so intensely that he longs for creation to be undone at least for him. He desires the magicians to rouse Leviathan to perform his work of undoing creation so that Job no longer lives and suffers (Job 3:8–10). God begins his answer by suggesting that creation is not undone or to be undone. God has created, has set boundaries to chaos and continues to sustain creation.[23] In this way God answers Job. Job ought not to wish for the world to be undone for him as God is still involved in sustaining creation. The world of which Job is a part exists as an ordered creation that replaced chaos. Job ought not to call for Leviathan to be roused up to create chaos as God has defeated and limited chaos.

However, the first divine speech does not simply affirm that God does control chaos and create order. God's manner of addressing Job offers a clue to the answer to Job's questions that is easy to miss. God challenges Job to be a warrior, asking him whether he defeated chaos at the beginning of creation and on this basis maintains creation. The answer is clearly negative. Job is not the divine warrior. However, in asking the question from the whirlwind of the theophany, God suggests to Job that the divine warrior who does conquer chaos has now presented himself without passing Job by for more important battles.

Job appears to miss the subtlety of this answer. His reply to this divine speech moves into the admixture of defiance and defeatism that often characterizes passive aggression. Job retreats into his theology of despair: "God is great and I am of small (read 'no') account. I was right all along. God celebrates divine strength and victory over chaos and moves in mysterious ways but I am unlikely ever to behold God's wonders. Doubtless God will perform them but somewhere else and for somebody else. God is simply too big to care about me as an individual and in the greater scheme of things my righteousness does not really matter." There it is. Reality is as bad as Job thought. God is all-powerful and might is right. God has chaos

---

23. This observation is not dissimilar from that of Habel (*Job*, 530–33). However, the table of parallels he makes in support of the observation contains some that seem strained (e.g., reading the theophany in Job 9:5–7 as evidence of the world falling apart). The observation rings true but only at a general level, there does not seem to be a systematic refutation of Job's earlier statements here. Rather God addresses his theology and states unequivocally that God *is* active in creation and *did* create out of chaos. Mobley (*Return*, 121–23) suggests something very similar, arguing that God answers comments about the design of creation made by Job and his friends but offers too few examples to fully substantiate his argument.

under control so Job cannot even die. The only appropriate response is silence.

God does not leave it there, however. This is noteworthy. If God had wished to silence Job into submissive acceptance of divine sovereignty, then there was no need to speak again. Why does God speak again? Possibly God is a monster and wants to drive the divine victim to the edge of despair and beyond. Reading the book this darkly is doubtless possible but fails to explain the extraordinary statement of Job 42:7 where God commends Job for speaking rightly.[24] Whatever one makes of the prehistory of the current text of Job, the text as it stands contains this commendation and the interpreter must come to terms with it.[25] If God were a monster who was insistent in driving Job into the ground as if he were Rahab or Leviathan, God would be very unlikely to commend Job in this way and restore him as God does.

God Versus (?) Job: Round Two

The answer to why God speaks again must lie in the content of the second divine speech. God begins by challenging Job again to gird up his loins like a warrior (Job 40:7). God now focuses in on this challenge, asking Job if he is capable of defeating the forces of evil in the way in which God does. God challenges Job to come in theophany himself and restore righteousness and justice to the world (Job 40:9–14).[26]

> Have you an arm like God, and can you thunder with a voice like his? Deck yourself with majesty and dignity; clothe yourself with glory and splendor. Pour out the overflowings of your anger, and look on all who are proud, and abase them. Look on all who are

24. Clines (*Job 38–42*, 1202–3) finds the God of the divine speeches rather "unlovely and not a little chilling." On his reading, I can understand this. Clines solution to the conundrum of Job 42:7 (Job has spoken rightly) is that God agrees that there this is no principle of retribution operating in the universe (*Job 38–42*, 1241). This seems a peculiar argument given that God immediately goes on to reward Job for his righteousness. This fact renders Clines' reading unpersuasive.

25. Any theory that suggests that originally the speeches and prose story existed separately and that this accounts for the discrepancy founders on the fact that a redactor redacts. If there were two different tales about a character called Job who suffered, and they had such wildly different stories about how Job spoke (violently in one and peacefully or rightly in the other), why did they not edit out the discrepancies between the two texts? I prefer to stick with the fact that we have one text and must interpret it as it stands.

26. Habel, *Job*, 562–63.

proud, and bring them low; tread down the wicked where they stand. Hide them all in the dust together; bind their faces in the world below. Then I will also acknowledge to you that your own right hand can give you victory.

God tells Job plainly that if he can do this, then God will admit that he, Job, has every right to have spoken as he has done (Job 40:8, 14). God challenges Job to do what only God can do.

Then God shows Job the chaos monster Behemoth (Job 40:15–24).[27]

Look at Behemoth, which I made just as I made you; it eats grass like an ox. Its strength is in its loins, and its power in the muscles of its belly. It makes its tail stiff like a cedar; the sinews of its thighs are knit together. Its bones are tubes of bronze, its limbs like bars of iron. It is the first of the great acts of God—only its Maker can approach it with the sword. For the mountains yield food for it where all the wild animals play. Under the lotus plants it lies, in the covert of the reeds and in the marsh. The lotus trees cover it for shade; the willows of the wadi surround it. Even if the river is turbulent, it is not frightened; it is confident though Jordan rushes against its mouth. Can one take it with hooks or pierce its nose with a snare?

Having surveyed the prowess and strength of the celestial monster, God asks whether any human can defeat Behemoth, confident the answer is in the negative (Job 40:24). God has already asserted that only he can approach Behemoth with the sword (Job 40:19). The implication is that God can defeat Behemoth. Indeed, God created Behemoth right at the beginning of creation and so has complete control over this monster.

God then does the same with Leviathan (Job 41:1–34). He asks Job a series of questions about whether he can capture or kill this monster (Job 41:1–7).

Can you draw out Leviathan with a fishhook, or press down its tongue with a cord? Can you put a rope in its nose, or pierce its jaw with a hook? Will it make many supplications to you? Will it speak soft words to you? Will it make a covenant with you to be taken as your servant forever? Will you play with it as with a bird, or will you put it on leash for your girls? Will traders bargain over it? Will they divide it up among the merchants? Can you fill its skin with harpoons, or its head with fishing spears?

27. For the identity of Behemoth and Leviathan as chaos monsters, see Day, *God's Conflict*, 62–87; Habel, *Job*, 557–61.

God answers the question. No mortal would dare because Leviathan is far too powerful for them (Job 41:8–14).

> Lay hands on it; think of the battle; you will not do it again! Any hope of capturing it will be disappointed; were not even the gods overwhelmed at the sight of it? No one is so fierce as to dare to stir it up. Who can stand before it? Who can confront it and be safe?— under the whole heaven, who? I will not keep silence concerning its limbs, or its mighty strength, or its splendid frame. Who can strip off its outer garment? Who can penetrate its double coat of mail? Who can open the doors of its face?

God describes in great detail the ferocity of this monster and how easily it defends itself against attack (Job 40:12–34). The speech seems to end on an oddly negative note: "On earth it has no equal, a creature without fear. It surveys everything that is lofty; it is king over all that are proud" (Job 40:33–34). God leaves Job with the strength and invincibility of Leviathan hanging in the air but God does not leave him helpless. God leaves Job with a question that has been repeated throughout this speech (Job 41:10–11, 13–14): who can conquer Leviathan?

At this point the penny drops. Job cannot defeat chaos. In fact, in the face of chaos Job wants to be swallowed up entirely by it (Job 3:8). After all, he is helpless before it. Job cannot come in theophany and restore justice and righteousness to the earth—the balance and order in creation of which the wisdom tradition speaks. Only God can come in theophany—Job has affirmed this throughout, although in irony and bitterness. Only God can defeat Behemoth. God has told us this. The whole tradition speaks out the answer to the question with which God leaves Job. Only God can defeat Leviathan.

Job retraces his steps in his conversation with God. God asked who darkened counsel without knowledge (Job 38:2). Having previously given a very negative response, Job now suggests that he had not understood what he was talking about. He claims to have spoken in ignorance of marvels he scarcely understood (Job 42:3). Exactly what marvels Job refers to here may be the subject of some discussion but his ironic and sarcastic use of the divine warrior traditions would certainly fit this description.[28] Job's bitterness

---

28. See the discussion in Clines (*Job 38–42*, 1214–15). Clines reads this verse as Job's ultimate act of despair as Job gives in to the divine "justice" against which he has railed so rightly for so long. If Job does refer to the marvels of the cosmic portents that accompany the divine warrior and his conquest of chaos here, as I suggest, then Job speaks plainly. He has spoken frequently of these things which God has brought up in both

prevented him from seeing the reality of the things of which he spoke when he described angrily and sarcastically God coming in the theophany of the divine warrior. Next Job recalls the challenge of God to listen as God speaks, which prefaced both divine speeches (Job 38:3; 40:7). Reflecting on the dialogue Job now claims that he has seen God. Previously he knew about God and the language of his coming in theophany to destroy chaos but now he has seen God come in the longed for theophany (Job 40:5). So Job decides to drop his mourning: "Therefore I reject and change my mind about dust and ashes."[29]

Hence the change of mood. Job has suddenly become excited about God. He claims to have seen the redeemer he was demanding to see earlier in the speeches or at least an acceptable equivalent in the appearance of God (Job 19:25–7). Why does Job respond so positively to God telling him that only God can defeat chaos and while Job remains seated in dust, ashes, and misery?[30] God has already affirmed that creation is not undone and chaos has been defeated. However, the theme of creation out of chaos was quite subtle in this first speech. In the second speech God is more direct. Only God can defeat Behemoth. No human being can defeat Leviathan—the implication being that only God can conquer this monster. Only God comes in theophany to restore justice and peace. God speaks this message out of the whirlwind. God has come in theophany. Both in his words and in the manner of his appearance, God shows Job that he has come to rescue

---

divine speeches. However, Job has spoken previously in anger because God seemed to have failed him. As Job now recognizes God coming in the theophany to rescue him, he realizes that there was more truth to the theophanic language he has been using to fire vitriol at God than he realized at the time. Hence, he comments that he spoke of things that he did not understand—because at the time he did not see their reality.

29. The translation of verse 6 is a moot point amongst commentators. Translations often supply the pronoun *myself* and have Job say "I reject myself and repent in dust and ashes"? However, the Hebrew does not supply any suggestion that Job is the object of the verb "reject." Dale Patrick ("Translation") made the plausible suggestion that "dust and ashes" is the object of "reject." He also noted that the verb and pronoun often translated "repent" and "upon/in" taken together can mean "change my mind about" (e.g., Exod 32:12, 14; 2 Sam 14:16; 1 Chr 21:25; Jer 18:8; 26:13). Therefore he suggested that Job rejects and changes his mind about his dust and ashes. Habel (*Job*, 576) follows this translation. Clines (*Job 38–42*, 1209) rejects this translation as Job cannot repent his dust and ashes as they are hardly something of which he need be ashamed. However, rejecting and changing his mind about (or repenting) his dust and ashes is an entirely appropriate reaction if Job believes that the God who destroys chaos has come to bring creation and order back to his life.

30. Presumably—so Clines, *Job 38–42*, 1234.

and restore him and Job suddenly sees it. This is precisely what Job was after and precisely what God does (Job 42:10).[31] God appeared in court and vindicated Job. Job had his day in court and won his case.

THINKING IT THROUGH

So Job wins his case and God wins his bet. (*Pause.*) Surely there is more to the book of Job than that? There probably is. The ending makes no mention of God winning his bet but the reader knows what he has done. Job does not curse God. He rails at God, complains that God will not treat him properly, and challenges God for failing to bless him. However, he does not curse God. God does win his bet against the satan but the author makes no mention of it. By the end of the story it is no longer important enough to mention. The focus is on God and Job.

Having allowed Job to suffer, God now asks him to pray for his friends, which Job does (Job 42:7–9). At this point God restores Job's fortunes (Job 42:10). The order in which things occur suggests that God tests Job's righteousness one final time before restoring his wealth.[32] The test continues. The friends have hardly proved themselves helpful or even willing to listen, let alone think. They have been insensitive to Job's needs. To pray for their restoration asks for Job to show remarkable grace. This he does and passes the test. Throughout the book of Job, even when salvation has been announced, God tests Job. God wants to prove Job's wholehearted devotion. At the heart of the book lies the challenging question: do you really love God for what you can get or do you really love God for God?

Job may confuse people and even cause revulsion because the question is so challenging. We can have a tendency to understand God more in terms of his duties towards us than our duties towards God. Any covenant

---

31. I was taught as an undergraduate to reject the rewarding of Job in the epilogue as a later and banal ending to the book, and was encouraged to prefer the Job of the speeches who was held up as something of a proto-existentialist who remained aghast at the abysmal which lies at the heart of reality. Much as I can see that theologies that seek a naively happy ending engage in the kind of denial of reality that debases those who suffer, I suspect that many who suffer would like their sufferings to end if they really believed it were possible. It is perhaps easier to justify reading the text existentially from an armchair in a Western university than it is from a shanty town community center. I am reminded of the comment of friends who lived in the shanty towns of Lima, Peru: "we are amazed that you Western missionaries long to be poor like us so you can feel like you are identifying with us. We do not want to be poor. We want to be rich like you."

32. Similarly Clines, *Job 38–42*, 1235; against Habel, *Job*, 584.

we have with God must bring us benefits or we do not deem it worth the trouble. Any God who demands without giving we deem unloving and therefore not worthy of praise. But God is God—both by nature and by definition to be worshipped. Job asks us to look deep inside ourselves and ask whether we worship because God is God or because God is good. The question can be unsettling.

But God is also good, although his goodness may be hidden and inexplicable. The narrative framework of God making a bet with the satan offers a setting for the speeches that mean Job really has no idea of what is going on. His suffering seems inexplicable. He has no idea he is being tested. He believes in a God who creates order out of chaos but experiences God as creating chaos out of order. He longs to know what this is about and how it may be justified, if at all. In the struggle of working this through, we uncover the spiritual riches of the text as Job lives with suffering and God.

Job begins by trying to sweat it out in accepting piety but his suffering corrodes his ability to sustain this and eventually he snaps. However, he does not curse God or others. He curses the day he was born and longs to die. His experience of chaos leads him to beg for chaos to engulf him in death—as the only the way out. His sense of defeat turns to anger as he lashes out at God for treating him like evil itself as his sense of justice drives him to ask the question of why God could allow such injustice to happen. He toys momentarily with the idea that maybe God does not actually care for people and suggests that maybe all God cares about is power. Reflecting some more, he muses that God probably does care for and save people—just not Job himself. But Job does not allow the distance he feels God has put between them to prevent him from approaching God. Right up to the point where he falls silent he challenges God to come and explain what is happening.

Job shows no signs of being afraid to pray openly and honestly about his experience. Job seems to understand his innocence and there is no suggestion in the book that he is anything other than righteous. Job is unafraid to talk frankly with his friends about his experience, even though it challenges their theology to the point where they cannot accept it. This is probably why God says Job has spoken rightly (Job 42:7). Job never allowed his dignity to be crushed under a theology that was less than true. Job was honest about who he was as a person, honest about how righteously he lived (and willing to hear genuine evidence to the contrary), and honest about how he felt in his suffering. Even in his darkest moments, Job had integrity and self-respect. In this sense, Job models righteous suffering. He struggles to understand, expects God to act justly, examines himself, and tries to hold onto the hope that God will one day hear him and intervene. Job is open, honest, and faithful.

The book begins with God calling Job "my servant" and the book ends with God calling him the same (Job 1:8; 2:3; 42:7–8). For all the thundering from the whirlwind about darkening counsel without knowledge, God seems to approve of Job who struggles with understanding the ways of God in the light of his experience. God commends him in contrast to his friends who will not acknowledge the reality of the chaos or allow for anyone to question. God takes Job's irony, sarcasm, bitterness, and resentment before finally revealing himself to Job in the storm. God hears the anger, disappointment, and despair and finally proves true to the old description of the warrior who will defeat chaos. This story of divine testing can only make us uncomfortable. The possibility that God might test us through suffering is unattractive. However, the book of Job speaks of a God who, beyond our darkest doubts and disappointments, rescues and restores the righteous, and encourages those suffering unjustly to bring their experience before God in honesty and integrity, challenging God to be true to his word.

5

TALKING BACK TO TRADITION
Matthew Transforms Theophany

ONCE UPON A TIME, in places we know and at times not too far from our own, people used to be told to pull themselves together. When crises occurred and people responded by lamenting their lot, others might be heard telling them to pull their socks up. These "others," in the minds of some today, have all the pastoral sensitivity of our mythical dragons—and some of those "some" might wish these "others" into the mythical past alongside our dragons. You might easily think that the ways in which biblical writers used our myth should encourage contemporary people of faith to rediscover biblical practices of lament. You would probably be right in thinking this but this is by no means the whole story.

The early Christians were clearly not entirely convinced about an indiscriminate use of the myth for wailing about our woes to the world. They picture Jesus as gently censuring this practice and teaching another way of handling trouble—and they use the myth to make their point. They talk back to the tradition. The gospel writer Matthew tells two stories in which he explores the spirituality of the tradition and pictures Jesus as trying to teach the disciples to handle their crises with more practical faith than panic. Matthew distils this teaching into stories about storms at sea. The first asks a question to which the second provides an answer and so the two are best read and studied alongside each other.[1]

---

1. There are various echoes of the stilling of the storm (Matt 8:23–7) in the walking

STILLING THE STORM

Matthew tells his first story in a way that paints Jesus as the divine warrior who rescues his disciples from chaos and death. However, his story is nuanced to bring out further aspects of spirituality and discipleship (Matt 8:23–27). Famously Matthew places this story after two stories about the cost of following Jesus in which Jesus spells out the cost of discipleship (Matt 8:18–22).[2] He then begins his story of the stilling of the storm with the telling phrase that Jesus' disciples follow him into the boat. At one level this simply refers to their getting into the boat with him. However, the use of the verb "follow" (which Matthew uses particularly of discipleship) and the term "disciples," after two stories about the cost of discipleship, signals that at another level Matthew uses this story to teach about discipleship.[3]

> And when he got into the boat, his disciples followed him. And behold there was a great earthquake in the sea, so great that the boat was being swamped by the waves; but he was asleep. And they went and woke him up, saying, "Lord, save us! We are perishing!" And he said to them, "Why are you so timid, you of little faith?" Then he got up and rebuked the winds and the sea; and there was a great calm. The people were amazed, saying, "What sort of person is this guy, that even the winds and the sea obey him?"

---

on the water episode (Matt 14:22–33), which suggest that Matthew wanted these stories to be read together. There is a storm at sea in both stories. Just as the boat may sink (Matt 8:24) so Peter begins to sink (Matt 14:30). Just as the disciples beg Jesus to save them (Matt 8:25), Peter cries out for Jesus to save him (Matt 14:30). The words of his cry "Lord, save me" are identical to those of the disciples in the earlier story ("Lord, save"), except that he personalizes it for Peter. Just as Jesus rebukes the disciples for their little faith (Matt 8:26), so he rebukes Peter (Matt 14:31) using exactly the same term ("people/person of little faith"). Even the phrasing for Jesus' reply ("and he says to them/ him") uses the same terms. (All the terms quoted in English here are identical terms in the original Greek of the New Testament.) In both stories in Matthew, Jesus addresses his rebuke to the disciples and Peter from the center of the storm as it still rages and not by way of reflection in the calm after the storm. The story of the stilling of the storm poses a question ("who is this person?"), which the second story appears to answer ("the Son of God"). Matthew seems to intend his audience to place the two stories alongside each other and, given that most of the parallels are with the scene of Peter walking on the waters, particularly to hear this episode alongside the stilling of the storm. On the first story asking a question answered in the second, see Davies and Allison, *Matthew*, 2:69.

2. Davies and Allison, *Matthew*, 2:68–69; Gundry, *Matthew*, 154; Luz, *Matthew*, 2:20.

3. Bornkamm, "Stilling," 54–55.

The telltale sign that this is no ordinary nature miracle can be seen in what Jesus does to the wind and the sea. He *rebukes* them. People tend to rebuke people or other intelligent sentient beings. There is no point in rebuking inanimate objects. So why does Matthew have Jesus rebuke the wind and the sea? The answer lies in the use of the term "rebuke" (*epitimao* in Greek—*ga'ar* in Hebrew) in biblical writings to refer to God defeating the chaos waters (e.g., Pss 18:15; 104:7; Isa 50:2). When Jesus rebukes the wind he addresses it as a manifestation of chaos and defeats it.[4] Matthew paints the wind and the sea as the forces of chaos and evil and Jesus as the divine warrior who subdues them.[5] He reads the story of the stilling of the storm through a mythical lens to teach his audience about discipleship.

The disciples see the effects of the storm and worry. Matthew describes the boat as being covered by waves. How literal this could be and could the boat remain afloat are questions a perceptive reader might well ask.[6] Presumably there is an element of excited storytelling.[7] Although not mentioned at first, there is clearly some kind of windstorm alongside the waves

---

4. Similarly, Davies and Allison, *Matthew*, 2:74. Note that the wind has become part of the manifestation of chaos in some Second Temple Jewish writings (e.g., *T. Jud.* 21:9; 1QH x 27; xiv 23) as well as a weapon in the arsenal of the divine warrior (see further Angel, *Chaos*, 42–43, 55, 112).

5. Mark takes the same scene further in his version of this story. He has Jesus tell the sea to be muzzled (the Greek *pephimōso* in Mark 4:39a is correctly translated "be muzzled"). This appears to be a very odd way of addressing the sea, which might explain why translators rarely render its true meaning. However, within the myth it makes perfect sense. The forces of chaos and evil are represented as the sea and as the dragon that lives within the sea. Mark conflates the images and has the sea (as chaos monster) muzzled. If the audience understands the sea to be both the Sea of Galilee and the chaos sea at the same time, this otherwise odd word makes perfect sense. The sea is the roaring chaos waters that must be silenced and the primordial dragon whose terrifying jaws must be muzzled. Similarly Mark has Jesus tell the sea to be silent. The motif of the noisy roaring of the chaos sea can be found in other Second Temple Jewish literature (1QH x 27; xiv 23) as can its silencing by the divine warrior (Sir 43:23). On the roaring of the chaos waters in these texts, see Angel, *Chaos*, 42–43, 55. On the silencing of the great deep (and discussion of the textual variants of Sir 43:23) see Angel, *Chaos*, 77–78.

6. The Greek word used (*kaluptesthai*) means "being covered" or "being hidden," both of which suggest the boat as been submerged by the waves.

7. The same must be true of the Marcan version. The waves are tossing themselves into the boat and filling it with water (Mark 4:37—the waves toss themselves into [Greek *epeballen eis*] the boat so that it is filling up [Greek *gemidzesthai*]), yet Jesus is fast asleep in the stern at the bottom of the boat. If we take the description literally, by now Jesus must be under water in the bottom of the boat so how come he does not wake up? Mark is using colorful storytelling to make the point that the boat was about to sink but expresses this in a way that captures audience interest and raises a wry smile.

(Matt 8:26).[8] With all this weather threatening to inundate the boat the disciples fear that they are going to drown. Chaos appears to overwhelm them.

Their reaction is to wake Jesus up. At this point in the story Mark has the disciples rebuke Jesus: "Teacher, don't you care that we're going to die?" Matthew has the disciples respond rather differently. In just one word, "Lord" (instead of "Teacher"), Matthew turns their rebuke into a prayer.[9] They pray: "Lord, save us, we are dying." However, this is no pious prayer in which the humble servants make a gentle request coming from the quietude of their soul. Matthew has them cry out a similar prayer to that of Psalm 69. That psalm begins: "God save me because the water has come up to my neck." The psalmist compares his enemies to the chaos waters and calls on God to save him from them, and using the language of this myth calls on God to punish them. Similarly Matthew has the disciples cry out "save us!" from imminent death by chaos waters.[10]

Although Matthew captures it in just three words, the disciples lament their situation. The fact that Matthew has them echo the cry and situation of Psalm 69 (which itself laments a rueful scenario from which the psalm cries out for divine rescue) underlines that this is a prayer of lament. As in many biblical laments, there is also a cry of faith. The disciples' prayer ("Lord, save") implies some kind of belief that God will save. Addressing Jesus as "Lord," with its overtones of divinity, suggests some kind of faith that Jesus had power to do something about the situation. So the disciples address Jesus as Lord as they lament their perilous situation and implore him to save them.

At this point, Matthew turns the expected narrative on its head. Psalmists who lament in the language of our myth generally expect the divine warrior to turn up and for chaos to flee away. The waters dry up as they see him coming.[11] Matthew tells a very different story. The divine

8. Mark introduces this earlier in the story (Mark 4:37).

9. Davies and Allison, *Matthew*, 2:73; Luz, *Matthew*, 2:20; Gundry, *Matthew*, 155.

10. Davies and Allison (*Matthew*, 2:73) compare this cry to Jonah 1:14. However, the verbal parallels with Jonah are not exact. Moreover, Matthew has words that are very different from the Marcan equivalent (Mark 4:38) and very close to the cry of Peter in the walking on water episode (Matt 14:30), which does draw on Psalm 69 (Davies and Allison, *Matthew*, 2:508).

11. The Jewish contemporaries of Jesus and Matthew knew this version of the story as well as ancient Israelites. Just as the chaos waters flee at the advent of the divine warrior in Psalm 18 (vv. 14–15), so the first-century author of the *Testament of Moses* had the chaos waters do exactly the same thing when faced with the advent of the divine warrior (*T. Mos.* 10:6).

warrior arrives in the guise of Jesus waking up. However, he does not rescue the disciples from the threat of death immediately. Rather he opens up a conversation about faith.

Jesus asks the disciples why they are timid. The reasons for timidity are familiar by now. A storm is raging so wildly that Matthew has compared it in opening comments to a tsunami (a great earthquake making waves, v. 24). The waves are sinking the boat and the wind is clearly against them also. There are few reasons to be anything other than despairing. Jesus' description of the disciples as "of little faith" may not be entirely damning but does not appear to be entirely complimentary either.[12] Certainly, the disciples have fallen into classic lament mode and this entails crying out in some sort of faith, even if that happens to be an admixture of faith and despair—as is most likely the case here. Jesus addresses the disciples as not being wholly convinced of his ability to help and asks them why they are like this.

Matthew has Jesus open up these questions in the middle of the sea while the boat is still sinking and the storm is still raging. The disciples can hardly have found his timing perfect. Yet Jesus asks the question: "why are you so timid, you of little faith?" He questions their kind of lamenting faith. He seems to expect his disciples to see something more than they are seeing and to trust him more deeply. His rebuke (however gently given) implies that he wants his disciples to demonstrate more faith in him and to change their attitude, to be braver in the face of what looks like disaster (and perhaps to see through it).

Jesus' very next action gives reason for doing this. Jesus rebukes the wind and sea. Jesus demonstrates himself to have power over the forces of chaos. Matthew portrays him as God the divine warrior who is able to conquer all the storms of life.[13] But earlier on in the story also, Matthew dropped a hint about Jesus' power and authority over evil.

Matthew has a great earthquake take place in the sea. Although this clearly refers to the storm at sea, it is a peculiar way of describing a storm.[14] However, earthquakes are associated with the portents that accompany the

---

12. The idea that Jesus berates them for lack of faith must be wrong. Jesus does not call the disciples *apistoi* ("you of no faith") but *oligopistoi* ("you of little faith").

13. Luz (*Matthew*, 2:21) seems to miss the flow of the narrative when he says that the disciples pray and the Lord responds by creating a great calm. Mark has the disciples cry out and Jesus respond by rescuing them—prior to calming the storm. He does not do that until he has opened up the question of faith with them.

14. Davies and Allison, *Matthew*, 2:69.

divine warrior prior to his defeat of the sea or chaos monsters.[15] Matthew seems to play with this story and the tradition. The storm is depicted as an earthquake at sea but there is a clear verbal parallel with Matt 28:2 ("and behold there was a great earthquake") where Jesus rises in triumph from the dead. This suggests that Matthew plays with the idea of the earthquake. At one level it is the immediate cause for the storm at sea (Matt 8:24). However Matthew uses this language to hint at what is coming. Earthquakes herald God coming to rescue the faithful and conquer chaos. The verbal parallel with the triumphant scene in Matt 28:2 suggests that the earthquake here hints at God the divine warrior being about to wake up in the person of Jesus and calm the storm.

Now Matthew was most likely aware that others in the early Christian churches were telling this story and may also have been aware that others were telling the story slightly differently. He doubtless focused in on the details that were important to his purposes. His setting this story within material that deals with the life of the disciple and his opening line about the disciples following Jesus into the boat both point in the same direction: Matthew reads this story as being about discipleship.

Matthew hopes that contemporary disciples will understand what the original twelve missed. He recognizes that all disciples will enter times of life where the forces of chaos and evil threaten to overwhelm. He knows that disciples will turn to lament. He realizes that this will become the most appropriate form of prayer. However, he encourages his readers to look beyond their immediate situation. Matthew does not intend to trivialize people's troubles as the story through which he makes his point has the disciples facing death. He appreciates that it will be hard to see the signs that Jesus really can overcome chaos. The disciples see much more easily the earthquake that sends the tsunami to destroy than the earthquake that heralds the coming of God to save. However, Matthew challenges his

---

15. Scholars dispute the background of the earthquake. Luz (*Matthew*, 2:20) suggests that the earthquake represents apocalyptic woes, citing Matt 24:7; 27:54; Rev 6:12; 8:5; 11:13, 19; *T. Mos.* 10:4; *2 Bar.* 70:8. However, as Gundry points out (*Matthew*, 154–55), the words of Matt 8:24 "and behold there was a great earthquake" (*kai idou seismos megas egeneto*) is exactly paralleled in Matt 28:2 where the earthquake is "a sign of Jesus' majesty" (a parallel also noted by Davies and Allison, *Matthew*, 2:71). Moreover, the earthquake in *T. Mos.* 10:4 is clearly a portent of the coming of the divine warrior (Angel, *Chaos*, 121) as is the earthquake in Matt 27:54 (Angel, "*Crucifixus*," 314). Although *2 Bar.* 70:8 clearly refers to eschatological woes, it is at least an open question whether the earthquake in Matt 8:24 depicts an eschatological woe or some variation on the theme of the march of the divine warrior. The parallel with Matt 28:2 would suggest that latter.

audience to take their faith seriously: to believe that Jesus truly is God and truly does have the power to conquer chaos and evil. The parallel with the resurrection (Matt 28:2) is unlikely to be accidental. Matthew challenges his audience to believe as disciples in the chaos of this life that the Christ who has conquered death can conquer lesser forms of chaos in this life.

The audience of disciples must see what the disciples in this story did not. Much as they trusted God to save, they feared the storm: "why are you so timid?" Matthew seems to expect his audience to perceive in the chaos and overwhelming evil that threatens to destroy them the coming of God to save. This play with the earthquake image (picturing chaos and foreshadowing their rescue by the divine warrior) captures his aspirations for mature spirituality. The disciple accepts within the suffering that God will save and sees in and from the suffering that God will come. They have hope rather than despair in the worst of circumstances. From the midst of despair they look for their salvation, confident in their hope rather than fearing their circumstances.

Matthew also drops a hint of how he sees this happening. Foreshadowing what happens in his second sea miracle story, Matthew has Jesus open up the conversation about faith in the midst of disaster and before he has solved anything. He opens up the conversation by questioning the faith of the disciples. He will continue this conversation in the second sea miracle story and have Jesus model the way to grow in this kind of faith. This modeling of how to grow in faith is linked to the question the stilling of the storm asks ("what sort of person is this guy that even the winds and the sea obey him?") and the answer that the walking on the water offers ("truly you are the Son of God"). In providing this answer in the second sea miracle story, Matthew opens up a whole new way of understanding discipleship.

WALKING ON WATER

Matthew follows up these threads in the story of Jesus walking on water. Matthew tells this story quite differently from Mark and John.[16] Again, in the way he narrates this episode, his focus seems to be largely on discipleship (Matt 14:22–33):

---

16. See the parallels in Mark 6:45–52 and John 6:16–21.

Immediately he compelled the disciples to get into the boat and go on ahead of him to the other side, while he sent the crowds away. And after he had dismissed the crowds, he went up the mountain by himself to pray. When evening came, he was alone there. But the boat was already (many stadia) far from the land, tortured by the waves, for the wind was against them. And in the fourth watch of the night he came towards them walking on the sea. But when the disciples saw him walking on the sea, they were terrified, saying, "It is a ghost!" And they cried out in fear. But immediately Jesus spoke to them and said, "Take heart, it is I; do not be afraid." Peter answered him, "Lord, if it is you, command me to come towards you on the waters." He said, "Come." Peter got out of the boat, walked on the waters, and came towards Jesus. But when he noticed the strong wind, he was afraid and beginning to sink, he cried out, "Lord, save me!" Jesus immediately reached out his hand and caught him, and said to him, "O man of little faith, why were you double minded?" When they got into the boat, the wind ceased. And those in the boat worshipped him, saying, "Truly you are the Son of God."

Matthew intends his audience to hear echoes of the old story of the conquest of chaos by the divine warrior in the story. He pictures the waves torturing the boat, an odd term but one that possibly pictures the waves acting demonically to oppress the disciples.[17] When Matthew speaks of Jesus walking on the sea (Matt 14:25–6), he uses words that are found in Job 9:8 describing God conquering the chaos sea.[18] Matthew wants his audience to hear in Jesus walking on the sea the story of God the divine warrior subduing the forces of chaos and evil.[19] This also explains the subtle change of vocabulary when Peter steps out of the boat. Matthew has him walk on the waters—not the sea. Matthew carefully distinguishes between Jesus walking on the sea and Peter walking on the waters although both of them are clearly walking on the Sea of Galilee in the story. By choosing his words carefully, Matthew portrays Jesus' action as echoing the action of

17. Luz (*Matthew*, 2:318) interprets similarly, associating this with waters of chaos imagery in the psalms.

18. See Angel (*"Crucifixus*," 306–7) for a review of recent scholarly discussion of this point. For Job 9:8 as referring to the conquest of the chaos sea by the divine warrior, see Day (*God's Conflict*, 40–42; Hartley, *Job*, 171; Clines, *Job 1–20*, 230–31).

19. The fact that the New Testament only cites Job 9:8 here and in the parallel stories of Jesus walking on the water (Mark 6:48–49; John 6:19) strongly supports this—see further Angel, *"Crucifixus*," 306–8.

God the divine warrior but excludes any such reading of Peter's action.[20] Again Matthew reads a sea miracle story through the lens of our myth in order to explore how disciples live with suffering and God.

By drawing so many parallels between the disciples in the stilling of the storm and Peter in the walking on the water story, Matthew pictures Peter here as the typical disciple and encourages his audience to experience the story through the eyes and ears, thoughts and feelings, and actions and reactions of Peter.[21]

When Jesus walks on the sea, he acts as the divine warrior conquering chaos. Peter and the other disciples miss this entirely. Their thoughts do not turn to Jesus bringing to life the myth of Job 9:8. Instead they worry that in what is already a life-and-death situation, they are now being approached by an apparition of the spirit of one already dead (possibly coming to greet them as they share the phantom's fate). Matthew gives no details of Jesus' appearance as he walks on the water but clearly he can be mistaken for some kind of ghostly apparition. The disciples see him but do not see him. They interpret what they see differently—and rather despondently.

Probably because he hears them screaming, Jesus calls out to the disciples. He tries to reveal to them his true identity. There is an amusing double meaning to the words he speaks. The Greek is capable of two translations. One is "it's only me"—in other words "don't worry, it's only me, Jesus." However, the Greek words are also capable of the translation "I AM" recalling the name of God from Exod 3:14. Matthew probably intends his audience to hear both. Those listening to the story might easily laugh— how could the disciples miss something so obvious? With the benefit of doctrinal hindsight the audience can easily see that Matthew depicts Jesus here as "Lord." However, those entering the story might experience things differently. How many times in crisis do faithful believers see apparitions rather than trusting that God has come in the person of Jesus to rescue and to save? The two translation possibilities pose questions to disciples ancient and contemporary: how do we see Jesus in crises? Do we perceive Jesus as friend who might come alongside us? Or do we perceive Jesus as the one who has the authority to change and transform our chaos?

20. There are no Old Testament texts that have God the divine warrior walk in conquest specifically on "the waters." For a review of the various arguments of this change of vocabulary see Angel, "*Crucifixus*," 307–8.

21. For the parallels, see footnote 1 of this chapter.

Peter nervously perceives the latter. He picks up the cue and recognizes Jesus as the divine warrior who can trample the sea. He turns Jesus' statement "I AM" into a question and a challenge: "if it is you . . ." He seeks confirmation of Jesus' identity as the god who conquers chaos. If Jesus can do this himself, he can work the miracle of Peter walking on the waters. So he asks for the miracle. Peter sees the challenge of faith implicit in Jesus' reply and he rises to meet the challenge. He wants to experience Jesus as God.

He steps out of the boat and all is well until he notices how bad the storm really is. Then he sinks. His understanding of the reality of his suffering and his closeness to death overwhelm him. His apprehension of his present suffering is greater than his understanding of the nature and person of Jesus. He looks at the wind and loses heart. He cries out as he sinks into the sea of chaos. Before the rescue, Peter turns to lament. When Peter prays, he takes his words from Ps 69:1: "Lord, save me."[22] The psalmist cries out to God to save them from drowning in the waters of chaos, and the terms Matthew uses of Peter crying and drowning are exactly those the psalmist uses in Ps 69:2–3.[23] Matthew wants to portray Jesus as the divine warrior conquering chaos and he wants to picture Peter as the disciple who cries out in prayer that God might deliver him from being engulfed in chaos and evil. The way in which Jesus rescues Peter by stretching out his hand may echo the picture of the divine warrior stretching out his hand to rescue the faithful disciple elsewhere in the psalms (Pss 18:10; 144:7).[24] Peter opens his lips in lament and Jesus saves him from drowning in the chaos waters. However, his rescue is hardly complete as he is not yet back in the boat.

We have no idea what the next scene looks like. All we know is that as Jesus talks to Peter, Peter is safe. Whether this means he is standing on the water, is up to his midriff in water, or is only just keeping his head above water remains a picture in the mind of Matthew to which we may never be

---

22. Davies and Allison, *Matthew*, 2:508. This is Ps 68:2 in the Septuagint (the Greek version of the Old Testament). The numbering of the psalms and their verses differs slightly in the Septuagint from in the Hebrew.

23. Ps 68:3–4 in the Septuagint. The terms are *kradzō* ("cry out") and *katapontidzō* ("drown").

24. Angel, "*Crucifixus*," 309; Davies and Allison, *Matthew*, 2:508–9; Luz, *Matthew*, 2:321 n. 48. Verbal parallels are lacking and so there is no solid evidence that Matthew echoes texts where the divine warrior stretches out his hand to rescue the faithful from drowning in the waters of chaos here. However, the motif would certainly seem to be present.

party.[25] One thing is certain, however. During his conversation with Jesus, Peter does not sink any further or at least not sufficiently more to drown.

Just as before in the stilling of the storm, Jesus poses a question of faith to Peter: "O man of little faith, why were you double-minded?" Jesus does recognize that Peter has some faith.[26] However, he also challenges Peter. The challenge is more specific than in the previous sea miracle story. Here Jesus asks Peter why he was double-minded. Jesus asks Peter why he looks *both* at himself (Jesus) *and* at the storm. This implies that he wants Peter to choose between the two. Will he continue to focus on his suffering? Will Peter allow his problems and difficulties to dominate his vision? Or will Peter focus on Christ in the midst of his problems? He asks Peter to choose between himself and chaos. The choice seems simple at one level but to anyone who has experienced genuine suffering it can read as quite stark.

The story puts the starkness of the question into picture form. Jesus may be standing on the sea but Peter is still out of the boat, surrounded by wild waves, battered by the wind, close to drowning but for holding onto the hand of Jesus and he knows that he has no capacity in and of himself to survive this situation. The question at one level appears absurd. Matthew wants the audience to picture the scene and to see the difficulty. He also expects the audience to look at Jesus. The wind continues to blow a gale and the waves are lashing around him. Nevertheless, he walks on the sea. Jesus is in control. He may not have conquered the sea yet but he is not being conquered by the sea either. When the disciples cry out, he speaks words of confidence and comfort. Jesus is calm throughout the storm. Matthew paints both sides of the question "why were you double-minded?" He asks the audience the same question, inviting them to look both at the sea and at Jesus and to reflect honestly on their own answers to that question in their situations of suffering.

However, Jesus does not make this call from heavenly glory. He does not declare from the divine council that disciples on earth must make this choice to concentrate on him and not their suffering. Matthew places Jesus

---

25. Although the psalm Matthew has Peter cite does speak of the water having come up to the psalmists *neck* in the Hebrew, the Greek, upon which Matthew draws, does not say this (Ps 69:1 [Ps 68.2 LXX]).

26. Jesus' reply has been described as a rebuke (e.g., Gundry, *Matthew*, 300) but Matthew has Jesus "say to" Peter and not "rebuke" Peter. The term seems too strong and Matthew knows the verb (e.g., Matt 8:26). It seems preferable therefore not to read this as a rebuke but as a question. How gentle a question it is impossible to say except that it is unlikely to be as sharp as a rebuke.

on the sea in the middle of the storm. When Jesus asks the question of his disciple to choose between believing in the storm and believing in him, he is present with Peter in the storm already. Matthew does not paint a picture of a distant God asking questions that place impossible demands on disciples. Rather, Matthew tries to teach his audience that Jesus is present in the storm with them and that he is in control and can be trusted—even if he has not yet conquered chaos.

So Matthew invites his audience to experience the story with Peter as the typical disciple and to hear how it speaks into suffering.[27] The storm represents chaos, evil, and death. The disciples are caught in the grip of suffering pictured as their being tortured by the waves. Jesus comes as divine warrior to conquer chaos but they do not recognize him. He does not rescue them at first. Rather he tells them who he is. He identifies himself as the one true God who can rescue them from chaos and death before he shows them this in practice. Jesus' self-identification represents something of a call to trust him. The disciples are on the edge of a dilemma. Peter acts in faith but flounders. Even in his lack of trust, however, he prays the prayer of little faith. Jesus answers the prayer of little faith in that he climbs into the boat with Peter and the storm marvelously disappears.

In all this Jesus invites Peter to live out a deeper and more trusting faith. Jesus invites his disciples to single-minded faith: holding onto the belief the one true God will deliver the faithful from suffering and evil whatever the circumstances. However, he does not teach his disciples this way of faith by rescuing them and their learning from this experience. Instead he meets them on the waves and stands there with him talking through their faith difficulties in the midst of their greatest fears. Matthew challenges his audience to stand with Jesus in their sufferings and learn through prayer and discernment the peace of a faith that simply trusts until salvation dawns.

Knowing God

Matthew takes the story and the spirituality further. He has Jesus compel his disciples to get into the boat without him and to cross the sea (Matt

27. Whether this suffering speaks directly to the alleged persecution of the Matthean church (e.g., Gundry, *Matthew*, 300) or not (Davies and Allison [*Matthew*, 2:513] are more ambivalent about reading a specific life-setting for this story in the experience of the churches to which Matthew addressed this gospel) does not affect the following discussion. My reading ought to work for both the specific suffering of persecution and for wider understanding of suffering.

14:22). Jesus has no intention of getting into the boat with them. He does not ask them to wait for him while he dismisses the crowd. He does not jog over the waves to catch up with them once he has dismissed the crowds. He goes to pray up the mountain by himself. Only when they are already in trouble in the middle of the storm does he take any interest in going to meet them. When he comes to them, he comes walking on the sea as the divine warrior of old. Matthew does not specifically say this but he seems to suggest that Jesus sends his disciples into the storm deliberately so that he can come and reveal his true nature as God the divine warrior to them.[28]

This suggestion makes sense when the two sea miracle stories are put alongside each other. The stilling of the storm ends with the disciples asking the question: "what kind of person is this guy that even the winds and the sea obey him?" The walking on water story ends with the disciples declaring: "truly you are the Son of God." The question of Jesus' identity raised in the first story is answered in the second.

However, the question of Jesus' identity is not so much a matter of knowing who Jesus is but knowing Jesus. Matthew does not picture Peter on the seas of chaos trying to work out who Jesus is and in what sense he might be divine. When Peter hears Jesus claim to be "I AM," he does not immediately launch a christological conversation with his fellow disciples in order to work out exactly how Jesus can be human and divine. Understanding Jesus' divinity has little to do with doctrinal formulations in these stories. Rather Peter asks Jesus to help him live in a new way. If Jesus conquers chaos and evil, then Peter wants to know whether Jesus will help him to live in such a way that he can pick his path through suffering successfully. Peter wants to know if Jesus has the power to rescue and save in his daily experience of living. Jesus seems to teach Peter that if he wants to rise above the forces of chaos, his focus has to be entirely on Jesus. The challenge to understand Jesus' divinity has become a spiritual challenge. Those who would know God must learn to trust that God will prove faithful from the midst of suffering and uncertainty. More than that, God is likely to take them there precisely to show them what they must do to learn to trust. God will take them into trouble precisely to teach them through that experience that God can be trusted.

28. Similarly Davies and Allison, *Matthew*, 2:501.

Something of a Challenge

Much as it challenges, Matthew's story at least has a happy ending. The dec-laration of the disciples that Jesus is the Son of God shows that they are at least beginning to understand. Mark tells the same story rather differently (Mark 6:45–52):

> Immediately he made his disciples get into the boat and go on ahead to the other side, to Bethsaida, while he dismissed the crowd. After saying farewell to them, he went up on the mountain to pray. When evening came, the boat was out on the sea, and he was alone on the land. When he saw that they were straining at the oars against an adverse wind, he came towards them early in the morning, walking on the sea. He intended to pass them by. But when they saw him walking on the sea, they thought it was a ghost and cried out; for they all saw him and were terrified. But immediately he spoke to them and said, "Take heart, it is I; do not be afraid." Then he got into the boat with them and the wind ceased. And they were utterly astounded, for they did not under-stand about the loaves, but their hearts were hardened.

Mark does not focus on the storm. In fact, he merely mentions an adverse wind which makes rowing difficult.[29] He does have the wind cease when Jesus gets into the boat with the implication that there is some sort of deliv-erance from what was preventing them from getting where they wanted.[30] However, Mark does not make the rescue theme as prominent as Matthew does.

Mark focuses almost wholly on the person of Jesus instead. He does have Jesus walk on the water using the phrasing of Job 9:8. He depicts Jesus as God the divine warrior walking over the sea in conquest of it. The idea of divine deliverance seems to be present in the motif of the wind ceas-ing when Jesus gets into the boat. However, Mark chooses to focus on the divinity of Jesus. He comments that Jesus wanted to pass by the disciples.[31] He makes this remark as he wishes to double underline the true nature

---

29. See Collins (*Mark*, 333) for a sobering and sensible critique of the tendency of commentators to read a storm into the Marcan text probably because they read this Mar-can text in the light of the Matthean story.

30. Ibid., 337.

31. This seems rather odd at first—out of character for the caring Jesus who seeks to meet the needs of those for whom he has compassion because they seem like sheep without a shepherd (Mark 6:34).

of Jesus as divine. The term "pass by" occurs in biblical texts where God comes in theophany and reveals the divine nature to someone. God passes by Moses in a theophany (Exod 34:5–6). God passes by Elijah similarly (1 Kgs 19:11).[32] Mark uses the tradition of theophany here.[33] He does not suggest that Jesus was going to ignore the disciples in their distress. Rather he suggests that Jesus was going to reveal his nature as God the divine warrior to them.

Mark underscores this point in his final remark in this story, that the disciples did not understand the theophany. Even though Jesus used words that echoed the divine name "I AM" in his response to the disciples, they simply did not understand the implication that Jesus was divine. Mark suggests that was because they did not understand what was going on with the loaves. This puzzling remark seems to recall the story of the feeding of the five thousand (Mark 6:32–44), which immediately precedes this story. There Jesus feeds the five thousand in a desert (Mark 6:32) just as God fed the children of Israel in the desert (Exod 16).[34] The feeding of the five thousand put Jesus in the role of God. The disciples did not see this and for the same reason they did not see the implication of Jesus walking on the sea.

The Marcan story presents a sobering commentary on discipleship and something of a challenge. Like Matthew, Mark has Jesus send the disciples to a place of struggle where he intends to reveal his identity to them. In Matthew they glimpse his true identity and respond accordingly. However, in Mark the disciples entirely fail to understand who Jesus is. Both evangelists tell the same story of faith but each presents a different possible outcome. Matthew suggests that those who meet Jesus in suffering

32. Collins, *Mark*, 334. The term in Greek for "pass by" (*parerchomai*) is found in all these texts. The reference for the Elijah story in the Septuagint is 3 Kgdms 19:11 LXX.

33. Ibid., 337 suggests that there is a note of anti-epiphany here suggesting that Mark recalls Job 9:11. Job does not expect to see God even if he passes by. She compares Job's belief that God will not lift a hand to rescue him to the disciples' not understanding. However, this parallel is so far from exact that it is better not to try to draw any parallel here at all. Job knows who God is and uses theophanic language to rebuke God for not saving him. The disciples do not know that Jesus is God and do not ask to be saved (from the wind). Mark (as narrator) makes the comment about the disciples lack of understanding precisely because Jesus is performing actions that should be read as revealing his person as God the divine warrior. The disciples consistently fail to pick up on the clues. It makes more sense to read the reference to passing by as suggesting the divinity of Jesus, which the disciples fail to understand without pressing the parallel with Job 9:11 any further than the fact that the term "pass by" denotes a theophany in both texts.

34. The Greek word often translated "deserted place" (*erēmos*) in Mark 6:32 has "desert" as its primary meaning.

will recognize his true nature and come to know him. Mark holds open the possibility that those who follow might meet Jesus in suffering, and even experience his saving them from their affliction, and yet fail to see or understand him.

Instead of knowing God in their suffering, they project their own fears onto the very God whose presence they need more than anything. They do not experience the presence of God in their suffering because they do not recognize Jesus as God. As Jesus is present to the disciples in their suffering, he comes as one who bears the promise of deliverance. The promise has not yet been fulfilled, but he comes with this promise. The disciples miss both the presence and promise and so are filled with fear and bewilderment. Mark tells a cautionary tale to his audience and asks them to consider their own response to the presence of God in Jesus in their own suffering: will they recognize the presence and the promise?

The ways in which Matthew and Mark tell the stories of the stilling of the storm and the walking on the sea suggest strongly that they are not simply telling stories but offering pastoral pictures to comfort and challenge readers to grow in faith in the risen Christ. Both present Jesus approaching disciples in the midst of their suffering and revealing his true nature to them there. The revelation of his nature comes as something of a promise that he will ultimately rescue although, particularly in Matthew, the revelation may come sometime before the rescue. The stories ask the disciples what they really make of Jesus. Do we believe in everyday reality that he can stand amongst us and transform our lives? Do we accept this even when he stands in the storms of our lives and converses with us without changing anything? The evangelists present different possible reactions.

Transforming Discipleship

But Matthew does more than this. He deliberately links the walking on sea story to the story of the crucifixion. He does this by means of a repeated phrase that links the two stories together. When Jesus walks on the sea and saves Peter from drowning, the disciples worship him and proclaim "truly you are the Son of God" (Matt 14:33). The cry of the centurion on the cross echoes this: "truly this man was the son of God" (Matt 27:54). Matthew uses the same words so that the cry of the centurion deliberately recalls that of the disciples.[35] Matthew wants his audience to read the story of the crucifixion in terms of the walking on the sea.

In the earlier story, Jesus walks on the sea and in doing so reveals his nature as God the divine warrior who rescues the covenant people from chaos, evil, and death. He rescues the disciples from the storm. Within the myth the storm represents the forces of chaos and evil. He rescues Peter from sinking into the waters of chaos when Peter chooses to step out and follow him as a disciple. Within the myth, the waters represent chaos, evil, and death. In the walking on the sea episode, Matthew teaches disciples that Jesus conquers chaos and evil, that Jesus rescues his disciples from chaos and evil, and that Jesus sometimes meets them in the storm and may simply be present amongst them for a while before rescuing anybody—and he teaches the disciples to trust that Jesus is still the God who rescues at times like these.

Matthew uses this declaration to link the walking on the sea episode with the story of the crucifixion. In making this link, he teaches disciples that on the cross Jesus acts as the divine warrior conquering the forces of chaos and evil. On the cross he rescues his disciples from suffering and death. Through his death on the cross, Jesus enables the disciples to step out and follow him and rescues them when and where they falter and fail.

But again Matthew makes more of the story than that. He does not simply talk back to the tradition but he turns the tradition on its head. Both in earlier biblical writings and in Jewish literature of the times of Jesus, people used the myth of their hopes that God would defeat their enemies and battle and bring them wealth and victory.[36] The tradition compares the enemies of the covenant people to the chaos dragons.[37] In the crucifixion scene Matthew does not compare the Romans to a dragon or the sea or any other kind of chaos monster—despite the fact that they act towards Jesus as enemies. Matthew does the opposite. He has an enemy recognize Jesus' true nature and so Matthew brings the enemy within the fold of Jesus' followers. Matthew has Jesus conquer mythical enemies whilst he is killed by his real enemies and at this moment he draws them into his family. In doing this

35. The Greek phrases are: "*alēthōs huios theou ei*"(Matt 14:33) and *alēthōs huios theou ēn houtos* (Matt 27:54). See further Angel, "*Crucifixus*," 304–5.

36. See further Angel, *Chaos*—especially the conclusion. A first class example of this would be column 12 of the War Scroll from Qumran on which see Angel, *Chaos*, 37–40.

37. For an example more or less contemporary to Jesus and Matthew, see *Pss. Sol.* 2:25–26, on which see Angel, *Chaos*, 83–86.

Matthew transforms the tradition from one of fantasy of conquest to one of self-sacrificial love for the other.

In making this link between these two stories, Matthew paints a very different picture of what it is to defeat dragons. Fantasies of conquest are blown away. Jesus changes the agenda significantly. No longer does the myth represent the fulfillment of desires or the acquisition of goods on the covenant wish-list: things God must give me if God is good. Rather the myth becomes about the giving of oneself for the other. Matthew leaves all this delightfully allusive. He merely uses a catchphrase link that asks us to read these stories in the light of each other. He does not (in these two stories) spell out the exact implications of all this for discipleship. But for all that, he certainly throws down the gauntlet. The cost of discipleship is much more than waiting for desires to be fulfilled.

Matthew talks back to tradition and transforms it. He knows the language of lament and has his disciples use it. He clearly affirms it because he has Jesus hear their cries and answer their prayers. However, Matthew does not stick in the rut of ancient lament. Jesus does not meet every demand of the disciples. He does not respond to order, even when cajoled. Jesus wants to teach the disciples to trust him more than they fear dragons. Matthew has him come to the disciples and to Peter and talk to them about their trust issues prior to rescuing them. He compels them to go into the storm so that he can reveal who he is and he asks their acceptance of who he is before he acts to save them (and so proves who he is). Jesus interrupts the lament with the question: will you trust me? He challenges disciples to move from the little faith that wails and cajoles to the faith that simply trusts. However, Matthew is not so naive to think that we acquire this measure of spirituality by anything other than trial and error. So he tells the story of Peter, who walks on water, sinks and laments again, and once again finds the faithfulness of God—and in doing this, Matthew tells the story of every disciple.

6

PLAYING WITH DRAGONS

THE BIBLE INVITES US to play with dragons. It introduces us to all sorts of people who have played the game before us. Although we may not always notice them, dragons can be found all over the Scriptures. When reading biblical books we tend to look for our favorite theological and spiritual themes and concentrate on the parts of the text that answer our questions—which is a perfectly natural thing for a reader to do. Most of us are not interested in dragons, relegating them to the mythical past as a whimsy not worthy of serious attention. However, the contention of this book is that we pass over biblical dragons to our spiritual detriment. It is worth seeking them out and seeing what wisdom can be gleaned from reading their texts.

Biblical authors were never interested in dragon myths for their own sake. If they had been, they would have bothered telling us the story many of them clearly knew (as they refer to it in various biblical books). However, they do not do this. Instead they refer to bits of the story. They play with these snippets, putting them in larger texts to make points about God and to make points to God. They use the story to describe how they feel about faith and what they think about their spiritual lives. They use the story to explore some fundamental themes of human spirituality and prayer.

Whoever wrote Genesis 1:1—2:3 knew the story. They also knew the situation into which they wrote. They understood how their community of faith had lost hope in their traditional faith. Exile in Babylon made it hard to believe in a God who promised to give the people prosperity, political freedom, and security in a land of their own. Those who had not lost faith appear to have been losing interest. A new poet-prophet proclaimed that God was stronger than the Babylonian God Marduk and would make good the covenant promises. The author of Genesis not only sang the same tune but wrote it into creation. Human beings are not the slaves of the gods— and if they are not the slaves of the gods, they are not the slaves of anyone else either. People were created to govern creation with God. This is written into the nature of all human beings because this is how God created us. This Genesis creation story calls the downtrodden and defeated to forget the stories (like the *Enuma Elish* for the exiles) that tell them anything different. It calls them to believe in their intrinsic value and in the intrinsic worth of all human beings. This author played with dragons to encourage people to be resilient.

The compiler of Proverbs looked at the same idea of defeating chaos in creation from a different angle and with a different message. God did destroy chaos in creating, and this has implications for human behavior. If human beings are to enjoy the goodness of the created order, they need to live wisely and according to the ways of the Lord. The author of Genesis 6–9 gave the flipside of the story. Where people break the boundaries God has built into creation, they risk bringing chaos back upon themselves, either through their own actions or in terms of divine punishment. These writers used the myth to encourage right living.

Other authors both inside and outside the biblical texts questioned this all too comfortable depiction of reality. Some suggested that God never did conquer the chaos monsters—that suffering and evil were simply part of life and that even God did not have them fully under control. Others seemed quite keen to put this idea down. The author of Daniel seems to write from within this debate. The imagery of chaos monsters is exploited. They are depicted in detail to give some kind of expression to the horrendous suffering of the people. The myth allows them to give vent to their emotion and despair as they wrestle with the promises of restoration of the traditional faith. At the same time the traditional story expresses the hope that God will intervene to restore. The story gives the space for questioning, for expressing negative experiences of faith and for exploring the spirituality of desperation at the same time as affirming hope. Part of its power lies in providing a framework within which to hold all the contradictions of spiritual life and experience.

The myth also helped the biblical authors to pray. The psalmists use the myth in a variety of ways. Psalm 74 looks back to the past from the disaster of the present and gives vent to anger. The psalmist prays with bitterness, disappointment, and deeply held anger towards God. They shout out the cry of their heart "how long?" Psalm 89 displays enormous resentment. Unlike some other laments, the psalm does not display plain and simple anger. Brooding bitterness feeds the construction of this performance. The psalmist plays with the genre of praising God for defeating their enemies and giving them power over them and uses the traditional language of defeating chaos waters to do this, before bringing the whole hymn crashing to the ground in screaming disillusion. Psalm 77 depicts the prayers of someone who has completely given up. The psalmist tries recalling the goodness of God in conquering chaos in the past but the psalm finishes before we know whether this has done the psalmist any good. There is an open-endedness about its praying that hints at expectation of better things but does not give the reader the happy ending. Instead it points to the fact that prayer can sometimes be a journey through suffering and the first step can be hard enough. By contrast, Psalm 144 offers the picture of someone able to praise in the midst of their suffering, throughout their ups and downs. The message and example of all these prayers (if there is one) is surely to pray openly and honestly. The script of God's goodness and commitment to the world is before us but there are many different ways in which we struggle through it as we find our voice in the drama.

The book of Job takes us in a radically different direction. It both explores the unfathomable mystery of the question "why does God not intervene to restore sooner?" and the life of prayer in the worst of times. Job's prayers are a masterpiece of honesty and irony. He moves from despair to anger. He gives up on God not by questioning God's existence but God's nature—asserting boldly that God does not care for human beings but is obsessed with power. He reaches the point of believing that God might be good to others but clearly does not care for him. Throughout all this he struggles with God, desperate to get some kind of explanation from God as to why all this has happened to him. Then God comes from nowhere and restores him. The book begs as many questions as it answers, but, again, the author uses the myth to give voice to the bitterest of prayers and the faithfulness of God. There is no explanation as to why God allows suffering, just an exploration of spirituality at the depths of suffering as someone waits on and gives up on waiting on God to save.

Matthew takes the story in a different direction. He plays the song of lament but turns it into a duet. He has God talk back. The disciples find themselves in trouble. They cry out for help. They want saving from their predicament. Matthew depicts a God who does save the disciples in trouble—but not immediately. Instead, he teaches the disciples that God can be present without saving and that disciples need to learn to accept, acknowledge, and enjoy the presence of God in the middle of disaster and suffering. They also need to learn to trust that God can save even when not currently doing so. They talk back to the tradition, asserting that there are two voices in any conversation with God.

So the biblical authors play with dragons. They do so in many different ways. They have no one-size-fits-all spirituality for suffering. Rather, from their own situations and predicaments they speak out. They all have the same script of God defeating chaos in front of them. They all react to it in different ways. Each author finds their own voice according to their situation and personality, or struggles to find their voice. If they give any example at all, it is that complete honesty about our lives before God is essential to living spiritually, and that working towards genuine openness to the work of God is equally important—even if one or the other is not always immediately achievable. They do not teach us how to play with dragons but they invite us to do so.

NOW DRAGONS ARE DEAD

This raises at least one difficult issue. The invitation may seem appealing. Spirituality can be stifled if not given the freedom necessary to be authentic. The attempt to imitate the spiritual patterns of other people often ends in failure. The beauty of the spiritualities we have been exploring is that they are open, free, and creative. Those who played with this dragon myth did so with the freedom that allowed them to live out a spirituality that was not only relevant but helped them enter fully into their own experience and read it in terms of their experience of and faith in God. However, they all used the language of dragon myths that have long since died out.

For most contemporary people of faith, trying to resurrect the language of conquering dragons in their prayer would be an artificial experience. It would most likely not be helpful as a result. Even within creative liturgies it might seem rather strange to ask God to crush the heads of the dragons in the ocean in order that a local political or international economic crisis might be resolved. For those who do not enjoy creative liturgy, the situation would only be exacerbated by the use of such language. It might be possible to get away with using it in hymnody where people of faith seem to be able to get away with most things creative on account of the freedom we enjoy in the arts. However, the fact that many of us might feel uncomfortable with using the language of dragons in quite the same way as our religious forebears did does not render the language either useless or dead.

Dragons may be dead but hopefully not completely. Much traditional religious language has been abandoned within contemporary faith communities on account of it seeming outmoded or naive. Talk of creation seems odd to many with the development of scientific understanding of the origins of the universe. Biblical and traditional descriptions of the soul have given way to the models of understanding the mind provided by modern psychology and philosophy. Yet religious people persist in assuming that God is responsible for creation. We also continue to use biblical and traditional language to describe the soul—and, ironically, there are scientific studies that demonstrate that those of us who are religious live longer and happier lives than most others.

Religious language and its use are complicated. We all know God is sufficiently great, that no description can quite capture God, and that this knowledge goes back millennia. Yet we try to describe God. Contemporary people of faith find themselves in a quandary as they struggle with the language of science and history on the one hand, and the language of faith on the other. We find reality in both and want to use both, and they do not always fit together easily. So we have discussions and debates about how best to do this. There are many suggested solutions to this problem. One such argues that we need to keep all our languages together, treating them as if they are real, with all their contradictions, until we find better languages to replace them. I think this one is a dead end for dragon language. We all know dragons are not real.

Another solution suggests we have outgrown the language of these sorts of myths but somehow we sense that they still have power to speak. So although at all sorts of levels we might object to the language (e.g., "dragons are not real"; "dragon language is violent") we know there is something useful there and we do not want to throw the baby of the meaning and spirituality out with the bathwater of strange and bloodthirsty ancient mythology. Therefore, we allow ourselves to become open to the power and the meaning of the language again. We know we cannot believe it like we might have done in childish fantasy worlds (if we ever did then) but we know we need to listen to and benefit from the power to speak into our experience of faith.

I strongly suspect that the biblical authors may have held a similar attitude towards dragon language. They show absolutely no sign of ever wanting to tell a whole dragon story. They rip the story apart to use the scenes that help them to explore and express their current experiences. They normally use the myth to describe something happening in the here and now, using its images as metaphors for their experiences—to say things that plain language cannot. After all, a picture is worth a thousand words. They do not use the language to describe the origins of the universe as if it were real. Whenever they link the language to creation, their main point is always about something in the here and now.[1] The biblical authors did not demythologize the story in the sense that they abandoned it but they do seem to have used it as a way of picturing and giving vent to their feelings as much as to their thoughts. It helped them to express both at the same time and in the same breath.

In this the biblical language of dragons has an advantage over the ways in which we most often speak of suffering today. Much as it may be legitimate to ask the question of how God can be omnipotent and loving and yet allow suffering, one also has to ask for whom it is legitimate or helpful to ask such a question. I would want to seriously question the usefulness of asking this question with very many of us in the immediate experience of suffering. The reason for questioning the validity of the question is simple. When we suffer, do we really want to know whether the existence of the biblical God is logically compatible with the reality of the evils in the world? I suspect not. When we suffer, do we want to tease out the various possible permutations of what divine love might mean or exactly how powerful God might or might not be? Again, I suspect not. I imagine that those who have committed to belief in the biblical God might end up asking these questions but only as a last resort. I wonder whether experience teaches us that when we suffer, we need to find a language of prayer. When others suffer, we need to sit with them and, if they give permission, offer them access to prayer. Locking people out of a language of prayer on account of making

---

1. This is even the case for Genesis 1:1—2:3, which is a call to resilience, and Psalm 104, which is a call to worship God and not the idols of Egypt and Ugarit. However, I am more than aware that there is a debate about this. On this particular point, I am sympathetic to the arguments of Watson (*Chaos Uncreated*) and Tsumura (*Creation and Destruction*) and less inclined to accept the arguments of Day (*God's Conflict*), who would link the myth strongly to the creation of the world as a kind of aetiological myth.

prayer part of an inaccessible theology that requires answers to impossible questions before one can access the spirituality it purports to describe is surely an act of spiritual cruelty.

Playing with dragons can help. The language of the myth is malleable. It describes the work of God in creating a wonderful world. God creates out of chaos and manifests untold love for humanity in not only giving us this amazing world but in making us partners in its governance rather than the slaves of the gods. The language affirms our humanity in the eyes of God. The myth can also describe the horrors of suffering, and the language of the myth can be developed to give full vent to the anger, frustration, fear, and revulsion to which suffering drives us. However, even at these times God is somehow in control and will bring resolution to the suffering. The language offers us the space to hold in tension our belief in God, our belief that God is good and the experience of our suffering. There is no need to deny any of these things. We simply inhabit the scene of the story that enables us to express where we are in prayer and the other scenes of the story will echo faintly around us. The myth gives us permission to be honest and real about our suffering without losing faith in God.

If the biblical authors held light to the reality of the myth, as I suggest, then there is no reason for us to take the language of dragons as anything other than metaphor. If they exploited this language for its power to express their lives of faith, then we might look for ways to express our own spirituality equally authentically in prayer. Like the biblical authors, we would be wise to use language that keeps emotion and belief together and that explores and frames them as part of the same reality. This will help keep our spirituality more fully integrated with our experience. We might also imitate them in their using a language that keeps together the despair of today with the hope for the future; hope, after all, is essential for living well through suffering.

Living in the Light of Eternity

This issue of hope raises a complex question. How far can mere poetry give hope? If it cannot guarantee a better future is it anything more than words? For orthodox Christians like myself this raises another complicated issue. Can we label dragon language metaphor, ignore the unpalatable bits, and then suck the marrow of what is left to help us find new patterns of praying in suffering quite so easily? Admittedly the language is metaphorical or mythical and biblical texts admit as much: for example, Daniel 7 translates the four beasts that arise out of the sea as four kingdoms. However, we cannot consign it all to the metaphor bin and then explain it in terms of human political, psychological and social forces and events.

The reason for this entails telling another story, which takes us back to Canaan and to the myth of Ba'lu with which we began. When Ba'lu received his temple after his conquest of Yammu, he found himself incorrigibly confident. This led in part to an argument with Mot, the god of death, drought, and the underworld. The argument turned into a challenge and the challenge became a fight. Ba'lu lost the fight and was swallowed by the god Mot—as is appropriate at the "hands" of the god of death and the underworld.

Isaiah (or a prophet from among his followers) knew this story and reworked it into a prophecy of God restoring the covenant people (Isa 25:6–12). The prophet paints a picture of the people of God feasting in joy as all suffering is taken away from them. The vision includes the comment: "he [God] will swallow up death forever" (Isa 25:8). The Hebrew word for death (*mwt*) is the same as the Ugaritic for Mot (*mwt*). In other words, God will swallow up the Canaanite monster Mot (the god of death) forever.[2] The prophet may have envisaged this literally or may simply have been singing a mythical song that was really all about God being faithful to the covenant people and restoring them.

Whatever the answer to that question, the story ends with Paul singing this old song for a new audience in his first letter to the Corinthian church. He proclaims that death has been swallowed up (1 Cor 15:54). He clearly evokes Isa 25:8.[3] However, his use of the prophecy has the robust faith of one who believes they are hoping in more than poetry. He utters the prophecy in excitement and praise at the idea that this monster will be defeated one day by Christ. He has reason to believe that Christ will do this at some point in the future as Christ has already conquered death in his own resurrection in the recent past. For Paul the myth of killing the monster has become real language about the defeat of death.

Accepting the resurrection of Christ as real, Paul suggests that the conquest of death (aka the chaos monsters) is more than merely wishful thinking and that one day death really will be conquered—but I recognize that the resurrection of Christ is the subject of no small debate. Even so, for

2. Blenkinsopp, *Isaiah 1–39*, 359.

3. Fitzmyer, *1 Corinthians*, 606.

those of us who accept it, the language takes on a whole new level of meaning as the story has already broken into our reality and calls for a response.

This then leaves us with a lot to take on board. The language is both metaphorical in some parts of the Bible and real in others. We cannot simply take the language off the page and re-use it. At one level we celebrate and look forward to the eventual disappearance of death. At another level, we decode the myth, treating it as simply a metaphor that somehow describes the action of God in saving, restoring, and healing people.

PLAYING WITH DRAGONS

So how do we play with dragons? What can we learn from this ancient myth for contemporary spirituality? I think the answer lies in inhabiting the story. I do not imagine that many (if any) reading this would contemplate believing in dragons any more than any of the people I spoke with that happy hazy summer's day when all the examinations were over. However, we do tell stories, real and fictional, that express how we feel and where we are. We share these stories with others and somehow they become a common bond between us that helps us to express our values, hopes, and identity.

The biblical story invites us to enter into it in this sort of way. We are not asked to believe in dragons. Nor do we need to spend time creating new versions of the old myth—though I recognize that some people who think and process very differently from me might find such an exercise useful. Instead we are invited to relate to the basic narrative of the myth. We are invited to believe that God has good purposes in creation, that evil sometimes dominates but that God will conquer suffering and death in the end. We are encouraged to recognize that some evil is inexplicably awful and that we cannot account for it, but that somehow this does not need to erode our faith in God. Rather, it should encourage us to be entirely open with God in prayer and whatever hope we may still have. We are given the freedom to dwell on one episode of the narrative in prayer with God if this is what we need to do. We are invited to be entirely honest about our own stories and open to the story of God.

The various ways in which the biblical authors used the myth invite us to reflect on our own situations and identities. They recognize that there is no one season in the spiritual life. They depict the very different ways in which we can react as we journey through pain and suffering. They demonstrate fearlessness in praying within and from each stage on the journey. They offer an example of not always focusing on the resolution but being honest about how we feel and what we think as we wait. They know the pain of giving up on any resolution and even giving up on God as having any interest in us. They give us permission to pray and lament in these places. At the same time, they bear witness to the belief that God offers a better life to all people and they encourage us to trust that God will write the alternative (and better) script of our lives into being. However, the biblical authors give us space to find ourselves in the story. They do not make these stories prescriptive. They simply offer pictures of others struggling with suffering and looking for the faithfulness of God and in doing this, they invite us to do the same.

The biblical texts that play with dragons are rich with spiritual experience, which helps us to open up to reflecting on our own lives of faith in meditation and prayer. Much as the language they use may seem quite foreign to us, it unlocks a spirituality of honest humanity in open relationship with a loving, but often very confusing, God. These texts encourage us to stick with this God in prayer and with a willingness to listen for God. They bear witness to the experience of our forebears in faith, that God does come—although sometimes only eventually. They suggest that when God comes, it is to heal and restore. They encourage us to believe the same and wait for God in our own suffering. They ask us to look for the needs of others in our suffering and to follow the example of the God who gave himself for others. They hold out a hope that one day this God will finally conquer all chaos and evil, and that we can be a part of that new creation. We may not believe in dragons anymore but perhaps the world would be a better place if we all still did.

APPENDIX

THIS BOOK REFERS TO texts that can be found in the Christian Bible and other Second Temple Jewish and early Christian literature. Below I give brief introductions to this literature and also bibliographic details of the translations of these works that I have quoted. These may be of use for anyone who wishes to read these texts themselves.

The Apocrypha or deuterocanonical books of the Christian Bible are a collection of books whose authority has been recognized by some groups of Christians at some points in history but not by others. Many early Christian teachers recognized their authority. Their non-inclusion in the Christian canon began arguably with Jerome in the fourth century AD. The Roman Catholic Church declared these books to be inspired and part of the Christian canon at the Council of Trent in 1546 AD. The various Christian denominations do not all agree on which books belong in the Apocrypha. The New Revised Standard Version of the Bible (Oxford University Press, 1995) conveniently lists which books are accepted as apocryphal by different Christian denominations in its contents pages. I have used the translations that are found in the New Revised Standard Version of the Christian Bible:

The Holy Bible containing the Old and New Testaments with the Apocryphal/Deuterocanonical Books: New Revised Standard Version. Oxford: Oxford University Press, 1995.

The Old Testament Pseudepigrapha is the name given to a collection of works that were in circulation in Jewish and Christian circles between the sixth century BC and the ninth century AD. These works are very diverse in nature. They are not considered canonical. The translation I have used for these works is the following:

James H. Charlesworth. *The Old Testament Pseudepigrapha.* 2 vols. London: Darton, Longman and Todd, 1983–85.

The Dead Sea Scrolls are a collection of texts that were used by a community of Jews preparing for the establishment of a radically holy and free kingdom of Judah in the first century AD, probably best identified as the Essenes. Not all the texts of the Dead Sea Scrolls were written by them but their library of texts helped them to practice the kind of holiness they were seeking for the nation. I have used the following translation of their writings:

Florentino García Martínez and Eibert J. C. Tigchelaar. *The Dead Sea Scrolls Study Edition.* 2 vols. Leiden: Brill, 1997–98.

I have used the referencing system used in this work to refer to the scrolls. In this each scroll is given a number (occasionally a name or letters). I have used this system so as to make it easier for anyone following up my references using the above work.

I have referred to but not cited works of ancient Near Eastern literature and also the Babylonian Talmud (a Jewish rabbinic work). Should anybody wish to follow up these texts, the versions that I have used to check my references are:

William W. Hallo. *The Context of Scripture, volume I: Canonical Compositions from the Biblical World.* Leiden: Brill, 1997.

Should anyone decide to follow up any of the references I give above, then I wish you the very best as you explore the fascinating world of ancient Near Eastern, ancient Jewish, and early Christian texts.

BIBLIOGRAPHY

Andersen, Francis I. *Habakkuk*. Anchor Bible 25. New York: Doubleday, 2001.

Angel, Andrew R. *Chaos and the Son of Man: The Hebrew Chaoskampf Tradition in the Period 515 BCE to 200 CE*. Library of Second Temple Studies 60. London: T. & T. Clark, 2006.

———. "*Crucifixus Vincens*. The "Son of God" as Divine Warrior in Matthew." *Catholic Biblical Quarterly* 73 (2011) 299–317.

Aune, David E. *Revelation 6–16*. Word Biblical Commentary 52B. Nashville: Thomas Nelson, 1998.

Baltzer, Klaus. *Deutero-Isaiah*. Hermeneia. Minneapolis: Fortress, 2001.

Barr, James. "Ugaritic and Hebrew *šbm*." *Journal of Semitic Studies* 18 (1973) 17–39.

Batto, Bernard F. "Creation Theology in Genesis." In *Creation in the Biblical Traditions*. Catholic Biblical Quarterly Monograph Series. Washington, DC: Catholic Biblical Association of America, 1992.

———. "The Reed Sea: Requiescat in Pace." *Journal of Biblical Literature* 102 (1983) 27–35.

———. "Red Sea or Reed Sea?" *Biblical Archaeology Review* 10 (1984) 57–63.

———. *Slaying the Dragon: Mythmaking in the Biblical Tradition*. Louisville: Westminster John Knox, 1992.

Beckman, Gary. "The Storm-God and the Serpent (Illuyanka)." In *The Context of Scripture, vol.1: Canonical Compositions from the Biblical World,* edited by William W. Hallo and K. Lawson Younger, 150–51. Leiden: Brill, 1997.

Berger, Peter L., and Thomas Luckmann. *The Social Construction of Reality: A Treatise in the Sociology of Knowledge*. Harmondsworth, UK: Penguin, 1967.

Blenkinsopp, Joseph. *Isaiah 1–39: A New Translation with Introduction and Commentary*. Anchor Bible 19. New York: Doubleday, 2000.

———. *Isaiah 40–55: A New Translation with Introduction and Commentary*. Anchor Bible 19A. New York: Doubleday, 2002.

Bornkamm, Günther. "The Stilling of the Storm in Matthew." In *Tradition and Interpretation in Matthew*, edited by Günther Bornkamm, Gerhard Barth, and Heinz Joachim Held, 52–57. London: SCM, 1963.

Boyd, Gregory A. *God at War: The Bible and Spiritual Conflict*. Downers Grove, IL: InterVarsity, 1997.

Christensen, Duane L. *Nahum*. Anchor Yale Bible 24F. New Haven, CT: Yale University Press, 2009.

Clines, David J. A. *Job 1–20*. Word Biblical Commentary 17. Dallas: Word, 1989.

———. *Job 21–37*. Word Biblical Commentary 18A. Nashville: Thomas Nelson, 2006.

———. *Job 38–42*. Word Biblical Commentary 18B. Nashville: Thomas Nelson, 2011.

Cohn, Norman. *Cosmos, Chaos and the World to Come: The Ancient Roots of Apocalyptic Faith*. New Haven, CT: Yale University Press, 1993.

Collins, Adela Y. *Mark*. Hermeneia. Minneapolis: Fortress, 2007.

Collins, John J. *Daniel*. Hermeneia. Minneapolis: Fortress, 1993.

Cotter, David W. *Genesis*. Berit Olam. Collegeville, MN: Liturgical, 2003.

Craigie, Peter C. *Psalms 1–50*. Word Biblical Commentary 19. Waco, TX: Word, 1983.

Croft, Steven J. L. *The Identity of the Individual in the Psalms*. Journal for the Study of the Old Testament Supplement Series 44. Sheffield, UK: Journal for the Study of the Old Testament, 1987.

Dahood, Mitchell. "*Mišmār*, 'Muzzle,' in Job 7:12." *Journal of Biblical Literature* 80 (1961) 70–71.

Davies, W. D., and Dale C. Allison. *A Critical and Exegetical Commentary on the Gospel according to Saint Matthew, volume I: I–VII*. International Critical Commentary. London: T. & T. Clark, 2000.

———. *A Critical and Exegetical Commentary on the Gospel according to Saint Matthew, volume II: VIII–XVIII*. International Critical Commentary. London: T. & T. Clark, 1991.

———. *A Critical and Exegetical Commentary on the Gospel according to Saint Matthew, volume III: XIX–XXVIII*. International Critical Commentary. London: T. & T. Clark, 2004.

Day, John. *God's Conflict with the Dragon and the Sea: Echoes of a Canaanite myth in the Old Testament*. University of Cambridge Oriental Publications 35. Cambridge: Cambridge University Press, 1985.

———. "Leviathan." In *Anchor Bible Dictionary*, vol. 4, edited by David Noel Freedman et al., 295–96. New York: Doubleday, 1992.

Day, Peggy L. *An Adversary in Heaven: Satan in the Hebrew Bible*. Harvard Semitic Monographs 43. Atlanta: Scholars, 1988.

Dhorme, E. *A Commentary on the Book of Job*. Translated by Harold Knight. London: Nelson, 1967.

Doran, Robert. *2 Maccabees*. Minneapolis: Fortress, 2012.

Emerton, John A. "Spring and Torrent in Ps. 74:15." *Vetus Testamentum Supplement* 15 (1966) 122–33.

Fishbane, Michael. "Jeremiah IV 23–26 and Job III 3–13: A Recovered Use of the Creation Pattern." *Vetus Testamentum* 21 (1971) 151–67.

Fitzmyer, Joseph A. *First Corinthians: A New Translation with Introduction and Commentary*. Anchor Yale Bible 32. New Haven, CT: Yale University Press, 2008.

Forsyth, Neil. *The Old Enemy: Satan and the Combat Myth*. Princeton, NJ: Princeton University Press, 1987.

Foster, Benjamin R. "Epic of Creation." In *The Context of Scripture, vol. 1: Canonical Compositions from the Biblical World*, edited by William W. Hallo and K. Lawson Younger, 390–402. Leiden: Brill, 1997.

———. *From Distant Days: Myths, Tales and Poetry of Ancient Mesopotamia*. Bethesda, MD: CDL, 1995.

Fox, Michael V. "The Epistemology of the Book of Proverbs." *Journal of Biblical Literature* 126 (2007) 669–84.

Fyall, Robert S. *Now My Eyes Have Seen You: Images of Creation and Evil in the Book of Job*. New Studies in Biblical Theology. Leicester, UK: Apollos, 2002.

Gaster, Theodor H. *Thespis: Ritual, Myth and Drama in the Ancient Near East*. Rev. ed. New York: Gordian, 1975.

Goldingay, John. *Psalms—Volume 2: Psalms 42–89*. Baker Commentary on the Old Testament Wisdom and Psalms. Grand Rapids: Baker Academic, 2007.

Goldingay, John, and David Payne. *Isaiah 40–55*. 2 vols. International Critical Commentary. London: T. & T. Clark, 2006.

Gordis, Robert. *The Book of Job: Commentary, New Translation and Special Studies*. Moreshet Series 2. New York: Jewish Theological Seminary of America, 1978.

Green, Alberto R. W. *The Storm-God in the Ancient Near East*. Biblical and Judaic Studies 8. Winona Lake, IN: Eisenbrauns, 2003.

Gundry, Robert H. *Matthew: A Commentary on His Handbook for a Mixed Church under Persecution*. 2nd ed. Grand Rapids: Eerdmans, 1994.

Gunkel, Hermann. *Creation and Chaos in the Primeval Era and the Eschaton: A Religio–Historical Study of Genesis 1 and Revelation 12*. Translated by K. William Whitney. Grand Rapids: Eerdmans, 2006.

Habel, Norman C. *The Book of Job*. Old Testament Library. Philadelphia: Westminster, 1985.

Hartley, John E. *The Book of Job*. New International Commentary on the Old Testament. Grand Rapids: Eerdmans, 1988.

Hasel, Gerhard F. "The Polemic Nature of the Genesis Cosmology." *Evangelical Quarterly* 46 (1974) 81–102.

Heidel, Alexander. *The Babylonian Genesis: The Story of Creation*. Chicago: University of Chicago Press, 1963.

Hillers, Delbert. *Lamentations*. 2nd ed. Anchor Bible 7A. New York: Doubleday, 1992.

Hossfeld, Frank-Lothar, and Erich Zenger. *Psalms 2*. Hermeneia. Minneapolis: Fortress, 2005.

———. *Psalms 3*. Hermeneia. Minneapolis: Fortress, 2011.

Humphries, Colin J. *The Miracles of Exodus: A Scientist's Extraordinary Discovery of the Natural Causes of the Biblical Stories*. San Francisco: HarperSanFrancisco, 2003.

Jacobsen, Thorkild. *Treasures of Darkness: A History of Mesopotamian Religion*. New Haven, CT: Yale University Press, 1976.

Jacobson, Howard. *A Commentary on Pseudo-Philo's Liber Antiquitatum Biblicarum: with Latin Text and English Translation*. Arbeiten zur Geschichte des Antiken Judentums und des Urchristentums 31. Leiden: Brill, 1996.

Kitchen, Kenneth A. *On the Reliability of the Old Testament*. Grand Rapids: Eerdmans, 2003.

Klein, Jacob. "Akitu." In *Anchor Bible Dictionary* vol. 1, edited by David Noel Freedman et al., 138–40. New York: Doubleday, 1992.

Kloos, Carola. *YHWH's Combat with the Sea: A Canaanite Tradition in the Religion of Ancient Israel*. Amsterdam: Oorschot, 1986.

Kraus, Hans–Joachim. *Psalms 1–59: A Commentary*. Minneapolis: Augsburg, 1988.

————. *Psalms 60–150: A Commentary*. Minneapolis: Augsburg, 1989.

Levenson, Jon D. *Creation and the Persistence of Evil: The Jewish Drama of Divine Omnipotence*. Princeton: Princeton University Press, 1987.

Lundbom, Jack R. *Jeremiah 1–20*. Anchor Bible 21A. New York: Doubleday, 1999.

Luz, Ulrich. *Matthew 1–7*. Hermeneia. Minneapolis: Fortress, 2007.

————. *Matthew 8–20*. Hermeneia. Minneapolis: Fortress, 2001.

————. *Matthew 21–28*. Hermeneia. Minneapolis: Fortress, 2005.

Moberly, R. W. L. *The Theology of the Book of Genesis*. Old Testament Theology. Cambridge: Cambridge University Press, 2009.

Mobley, Gregory. *The Return of the Chaos Monsters and Other Backstories of the Bible*. Grand Rapids: Eerdmans, 2012.

Mowinckel, Sigmund. *The Psalms in Israel's Worship*. Translated by D. R. Ap-Thomas. 1962. Reprint. The Biblical Resource Series. Grand Rapids: Eerdmans, 2004.

Murphy, Roland E. *Proverbs*. Word Biblical Commentary 22. Nashville: Thomas Nelson, 1998.

Nickelsburg George W. E., and James C. VanderKam. *1 Enoch: A New Translation*. Minneapolis: Fortress, 2004.

Pardee, Dennis. "The Ba'lu Myth." In *The Context of Scripture, vol. 1: Canonical Compositions from the Biblical World,* edited by William W. Hallo and K. Lawson Younger, 241–74. Leiden: Brill, 1997.

Patrick, Dale. "The Translation of Job xlii 6." *Vetus Testamentum* 26 (1976) 369–71.

Schaefer, Konrad. *Psalms*. Berit Olam. Collegeville, MN: Liturgical, 2001.

Smith, Mark S. *The Ugaritic Baal Cycle, vol. 1: Introduction with Text, Translation and Commentary of KTU 1.1—1.2*. Supplements to Vetus Testamentum 55. Leiden: Brill, 1994.

Smith, Ralph L. *Micah–Malachi*. Word Biblical Commentary 32. Waco, TX: Word, 1984.

Stone, Michael E. *Fourth Ezra*. Hermeneia. Minneapolis: Fortress, 1990.

Tate, Marvin E. *Psalms 51–100*. Word Biblical Commentary 20. Dallas, TX: Word, 1990.

Tsumura, David T. *Creation and Destruction: A Reappraisal of the Chaoskampf Theory in the Old Testament*. Winona Lake, IN: Eisenbrauns, 2005.

Watson, Rebecca. *Chaos Uncreated: A Reassessment of the Theme of "Chaos" in the Hebrew Bible*. Beihefte zur Zeitschrift für die alttestamentliche Wissenschaft 341. Berlin: de Gruyter, 2005.

Wenham, Gordon J. *Genesis 1–15*. Word Biblical Commentary 1. Waco, TX: Word, 1987.

Wyatt, Nicholas. *Religious Texts from Ugarit: The Words of Ilimilku and his Colleagues*. The Biblical Seminar 53. Sheffield, UK: Sheffield Academic, 1998.

INDEX OF ANCIENT SOURCES

INDEX OF MODERN AUTHORS